Collins

Student Support
Materials for AQA

AS Chemistry

Unit 1: Foundation Chemistry

FOR / 3 WK LOAN
REFERENCE ONLY

Authors: John Bentham, Colin Chambers, Graham Curtis,
Geoffrey Hallas, Andrew Maczek, David Nicholls.

William Collins's dream of knowledge for all began with the publication of his first book in 1819. A self-educated mill worker, he not only enriched millions of lives, but also founded a flourishing publishing house. Today, staying true to this spirit, Collins books are packed with inspiration, innovation and practical expertise. They place you at the centre of a world of possibility and give you exactly what you need to explore it.

Collins. Freedom to teach.

Published by Collins
An imprint of HarperCollinsPublishers
77-85 Fulham Palace Road
Hammersmith
London
W6 8JB

Browse the complete Collins catalogue at
www.collinseducation.com

© HarperCollinsPublishers Limited 2008

10 9 8 7 6 5 4

ISBN-13 978-0-00-726825-2
ISBN-10 0-00-726825-4

John Bentham, Graham Curtis, Andrew Maczek, Colin Chambers, David Nicholls and Geoffrey Hallas assert their moral right to be identified as the authors of this work.

British Library Cataloguing in Publication Data. A Catalogue record for this publication is available from the British Library.

Commissioned by Penny Fowler
Edited by Jane Glendening
Proof read by Patrick Roberts
Design by Newgen Imaging
Cover design by Angela English
Production by Arjen Jansen
Printed and bound in Hong Kong by Printing Express

Mixed Sources
Product group from well-managed
forests and other controlled sources
www.fsc.org Cert no. SW-COC-1806
© 1996 Forest Stewardship Council

FSC is a non-profit international organisation established to promote the responsible management of the world's forests. Products carrying the FSC label are independently certified to assure consumers that they come from forests that are managed to meet the social, economic and ecological needs of present and future generations.

Find out more about HarperCollins and the environment at
www.harpercollins.co.uk/green

Contents

3.1.1 Atomic structure

Fundamental particles

A nuclear physicist may claim that the true fundamental particles are *quarks,* but the chemist can develop all the necessary explanations for structure and bonding by assuming that an atom is made from the particles shown in Table 1.

Table 1
Properties of fundamental particles

Particle	Mass/kg	Charge/C	Relative mass	Relative charge
proton	1.673×10^{-27}	1.602×10^{-19}	1	+1
neutron	1.675×10^{-27}	0	1	0
electron	9.109×10^{-31}	1.602×10^{-19}	5.45×10^{-4}	−1

Examiners' Notes

The SI unit of charge is the coulomb (C). SI is the abbreviation used for the international system of units of measurement (système international d'unité).

The relative mass of an electron is so small in comparison with the mass of a proton or the mass of a neutron that it is often taken to be zero.

Protons, neutrons and electrons

An atom consists of electrons surrounding a small, heavy nucleus that contains protons and neutrons (except for ^{1}H which has only one proton and no neutrons in the nucleus).

Mass number and isotopes

Examiners' Notes

The atomic radius of a hydrogen atom is about 10 000 times the radius of the nucleus.

Definition

The **mass number, A,** of an atom is the total number of protons and neutrons in the nucleus of one atom of the element.

Definition

The **atomic (proton) number, Z,** of an atom is the number of protons in the nucleus of an atom.

An atom is neutral; it has no overall charge. The charge on a proton is equal but opposite to the charge on an electron. Therefore the atomic number must also be equal to the number of electrons in a neutral atom. In an element, each atom has the same atomic number, the same number of protons and the same number of electrons. **Isotopes** are atoms of the same element with the same atomic number but different mass numbers.

The notation for an isotope gives the mass number and the atomic number:

$$\begin{matrix} \text{mass number} & \rightarrow & 12 \\ \text{atomic number} & \rightarrow & 6 \end{matrix} \text{C} \quad \text{or in general} \quad {}^{A}_{Z}\text{X}$$

Some isotopes of hydrogen are $\ {}^1_1\text{H}\ \ {}^2_1\text{H}\ \ {}^3_1\text{H}$

Some isotopes of chlorine are $\ {}^{35}_{17}\text{Cl}\ \ {}^{37}_{17}\text{Cl}$

The number of neutrons in the nucleus of an isotope can be calculated as follows:

$$\text{mass number} = \text{number of protons} + \text{number of neutrons}$$
so $\text{number of neutrons} = \text{mass number} - \text{atomic number}$

e.g. for $^{12}_{6}C$, the number of neutrons $= 12 - 6 = 6$

for $^{13}_{6}C$, the number of neutrons $= 13 - 6 = 7$

The chemical properties of isotopes are almost identical, because isotopes have the same number of protons and electrons. Chemical properties are dictated by the number and the arrangement of electrons. The only differences between isotopes are in physical properties, such as rates of diffusion, which depend on the mass of the particles, or in nuclear properties such as radioactivity and the ability to absorb neutrons. Different isotopes of the same element also have slightly different boiling points.

Principles of a simple mass spectrometer

A mass spectrometer (Fig 1) is used to separate ions having nuclei of differing mass. It can also be used to help to identify complex molecules.

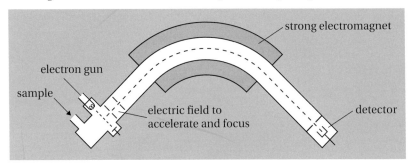

Fig 1
A mass spectrometer (simplified)

Ionisation

A sample is placed in the spectrometer and, if it is not already a gas, it is vaporised. The atoms or molecules diffuse into the path of electrons from the electron gun and are ionised. The gun fires high-energy electrons which knock out an electron from gaseous particles so that they form positive ions:

$$M(g) + e^- \rightarrow M^+(g) + 2e^-$$

This equation representing ionisation can be simplified as shown in these examples:

$$He(g) \rightarrow He^+(g) + e^-$$
$$H_2(g) \rightarrow H_2^+(g) + e^-$$

Some doubly charged ions (e.g. He^{2+}) may also be produced, but in smaller amounts because more energy is required for the electron gun to knock out two electrons. Molecules may also be broken into many different fragments by the high-energy electrons from the gun:

$$CH_4(g) \rightarrow CH_4^+(g) + e^- \quad (CH_3^+, CH_2^+, CH^+ \text{ and } C^+ \text{ are also produced})$$

Essential Notes

Fragmentation is considered in more detail in *Collins Student Support Materials: Unit 4 – Kinetics, Equilibria and Organic Chemistry*, section 3.4.11.

Acceleration

The positive ions are accelerated by an electric field and focused into a beam by passing them through a series of slits.

Deflection

The beam of fast-moving, positive ions is then deflected by a strong magnetic field. The magnitude of the deflection depends on the mass-to-charge ratio (m/z) of the ion. When m/z is small, the deflection is large.

Detection

The ions in the beam are detected electrically. When an ion hits the detector, it accepts an electron, and this creates a small electric current which is amplified and produces a signal on a computer. The magnitude of the amplified current is related to the number of ions that hit the detector and hence the relative intensity of the peak caused by an ion with a particular m/z value (see Fig 2). Ions with small m/z values are detected when the deflecting magnetic field is small. The magnetic field can be increased (or the accelerating electric field can be decreased) in order to deflect heavier ions into the detector one after another and thereby produce a 'spectrum'. A typical printout from a mass spectrometer showing the mass spectrum of a sample of chlorine is shown in Fig 2.

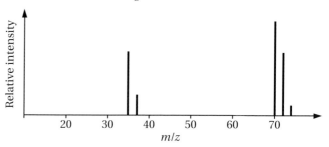

Examiners' Notes

Heavy ions have large m/z values and are deflected least.

Essential Notes

The mass spectrometer is sensitive enough to distinguish clearly between isotopes.

Essential Notes

A mass spectrometer can be used to identify elements from the m/z values of their isotopes.
  Elements that have an extra-terrestrial origin (e.g. those found in meteorites) often have a different ratio of isotopes compared with the same element on planet Earth.

Fig 2
The mass spectrum of chlorine

The peak at $m/z = 35$ represents the $^{35}Cl^+$ ion. The ratio of peak heights at $m/z = 35$ and 37 is 3 : 1. The peak heights for the Cl_2^+ ions are in the ratio 9 : 6 : 1. This ratio represents the proportions of Cl_2^+ ions with $m/z = 70$, 72 and 74, respectively.

The peaks in the mass spectrum can be assigned as in Table 2.

Table 2
Assignment of peaks in the mass spectrum of chlorine

m/z	35	37	70	72	74
Ion from	^{35}Cl	^{37}Cl	$^{35}Cl - ^{35}Cl$	$^{37}Cl - ^{35}Cl$	$^{37}Cl - ^{37}Cl$

The **relative atomic mass** (A_r) of an isotopic mixture can be calculated by using information from a mass spectrum. The spectrum above shows that the relative proportions of isotopes in that sample of chlorine are:

$$^{35}Cl : {^{37}Cl} \quad = \quad 3 : 1$$

so $\frac{3}{4}$ of the sample is ^{35}Cl and $\frac{1}{4}$ of the sample is ^{37}Cl

so $A_r = \frac{3}{4} \times 35 + \frac{1}{4} \times 37 = 35.5$

Examiners' Notes

For simplicity, the atomic number of isotopes is often omitted in symbols such as ^{35}Cl.

The *effective relative atomic mass* of an element is determined by calculating the weighted mean of the individual relative atomic masses of the isotopes. The *abundance* of the different isotopes is found from a mass spectrum.

The **relative molecular mass** (M_r) of a substance can also be determined from its mass spectrum. When a sample, X, is introduced into a mass

Essential Notes

For definitions of the terms A_r and M_r see section 3.1.2

spectrometer, provided that the molecule is not completely fragmented, the peaks near the maximum value of m/z correspond to molecular ions, X^+, made up from the various isotopic mixtures. The relative molecular mass of the substance can be calculated from these peaks.

Electron arrangement (configuration)

Electron arrangement in atoms and ions

It was originally considered that the maximum number of electrons that could be accommodated in the outside layer of an atom was eight and that these electrons occupied a circular or spherical orbit. The elements from helium to krypton were thought to be inert because their outer orbits were full.

This model of atomic structure has been replaced by one that is able to account for observed facts, such as the reactions of fluorine with these gases which are now referred to as 'noble' rather than 'inert'. In this later model, the electrons in atoms are arranged into main (or principal) **energy levels**, which are numbered. Level 1 contains electrons which are closest to the nucleus. Within levels there are sub-levels designated s, p, d, f. The maximum number of sub-levels is different for each level and is shown in Table 3.

Each sub-level consists of **orbitals**. Each orbital can hold a maximum of two electrons which have opposite spin. The number of orbitals and the maximum number of electrons which can be accommodated in each sub-level are shown in Table 4.

Main (principal) level	1	2	3	4
Sub-levels in that level	s	s, p	s, p, d	s, p, d, f

Sub-level	s	p	d	f
number of orbitals in sub-level	1	3	5	7
maximum number of electrons	2	6	10	14

Owing to differences in shielding from the nucleus, different sub-levels within a level have slightly different energies. A typical energy-level diagram for an atom is shown in Fig 3.

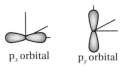

		(4p)	(3d)
level 4	— (4s)	——— (3p)	
level 3	— (3s)		
level 2	— (2s)	——— (2p)	
level 1	— (1s)	each orbital can hold up to 2 electrons	

Fig 3
A typical energy–level diagram

Level 2 sub-levels all lie below level 3 sub-levels but, in atoms, sub-level 3d is higher in energy than sub-level 4s.

The electron configurations of atoms of elements can be deduced from this diagram. Typical configurations are:

- Li $\quad 1s^2 2s^1$
- F $\quad 1s^2 2s^2 2p^5$
- Fe $\quad 1s^2 2s^2 2p^6 3s^2 3p^6 4s^2 3d^6$

Examiners' Notes

Main (principal) energy levels for electrons are sometimes referred to as shells.

Essential Notes

If electrons are regarded as clouds rather than as particles, the electron cloud has a characteristic shape for each type of orbital.

Table 3
Types of sub-level in each electron energy level (shell)

Table 4
Number of orbitals and maximum number of electrons in each sub-level

Essential Notes

An s orbital is an electron cloud with spherical symmetry.

The diagrams of p orbitals are shown superimposed on 3 dimensional x, y, z axes. Each p orbital has twin lobes.

p_x orbital $\qquad$ p_y orbital

p_z orbital

(The d and f orbitals have more complicated shapes.)

The electron configurations of ions can be deduced from the configuration of the neutral atom by adding or removing electrons. A complication is that, for transition-metal ions, the 3d sub-level is lower in energy than the 4s, so that the 4s electrons are removed first:

- Li^+ $1s^2$
- F^- $1s^2 2s^2 2p^6$
- Fe^{3+} $1s^2 2s^2 2p^6 3s^2 3p^6 3d^5$

First ionisation energy and electron arrangements

> ## Definition
>
> The **first ionisation energy** of an element is defined as the enthalpy change for the removal of one mole of electrons from one mole of atoms of the element in the gas phase:
>
> $$X(g) \rightarrow X^+(g) + e^-$$

The first ionisation energies of the Group 2 metals (Be–Ba) vary as shown in Fig 4.

Fig 4
First ionisation energies of the Group 2 elements

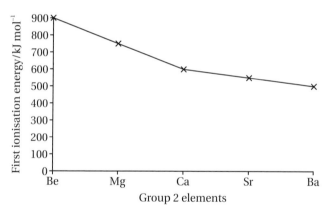

Essential Notes

A Periodic Table is printed at the back of this booklet.

There is a successive decrease in first ionisation energy from beryllium to barium. Magnesium has a lower first ionisation energy than beryllium because its outer electron is in a 3s sub-level rather than a 2s sub-level. The 3s sub-level is higher in energy than the 2s sub-level. The 3s electron is further from the nucleus and is more shielded from the nucleus by inner electrons. Thus, the 3s electron is more easily removed. This trend in ionisation energies is evidence for the electrons of atoms being organised in levels. A similar decrease in ionisation energy occurs down each group in the Periodic Table.

The first ionisation energies of the elements from neon to potassium vary as shown in Fig 5.

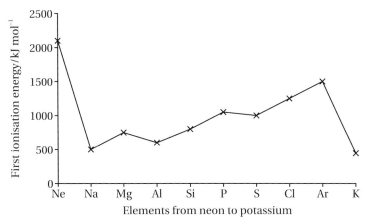

Fig 5
First ionisation energies of the
elements neon to potassium

There is a general increase in ionisation energy across Period 3 (sodium to argon). Across the period from Na (11 protons) to Ar (18 protons) the nuclear charge in each element increases. So the electrons are attracted more strongly to the nucleus and it takes more energy to remove one from the atom.

There is a fall in ionisation energy from magnesium to aluminium because the outer electron in Al (configuration $1s^2 2s^2 2p^6 3s^2 3p^1$) is in a p sub-level. The p sub-level electron is higher in energy than the outer electron in Mg ($1s^2 2s^2 2p^6 3s^2$) which is in an s sub-level.

The fall in ionisation energy from phosphorus to sulfur can be explained by considering their electronic arrangements (see Fig 6).

The 3p electrons in phosphorus are unpaired. If there are several empty sub-levels all of the same energy, electrons will organise themselves so that they remain unpaired and occupy as many sub-levels as possible. In sulfur the fourth 3p electron is paired. There is some repulsion between paired electrons in the samc sub-level, which increases their energy. Therefore it is easier to remove one of these paired 3p electrons from sulfur than it is to remove an unpaired 3p electron from phosphorus.

Examiners' Notes

The first ionisation energy of neon is greater than that of sodium because the outermost electron in sodium is in a main level which is further from the nucleus and more shielded. This big difference in ionisation energy from neon to sodium is strong evidence for the existence of main (principal) electron energy levels.

Essential Notes

Electrons have a property called spin. A spinning electron can be represented by an arrow. Electrons can only spin in one of two directions and are shown by up or down arrows, i.e. ↑ or ↓. The arrows represent the magnetic field produced by the spinning elcctron.

phosphorus: ↑ ↑ ↑ (3p)   sulfur: ↑↓ ↑ ↑ (3p)

⇅ (3s)   ⇅ (3s)

⇅ ⇅ ⇅ (2p)   ⇅ ⇅ ⇅ (2p)

⇅ (2s)   ⇅ (2s)

⇅ (1s)   ⇅ (1s)

Fig 6
Energy levels for phosphorus and sulfur

Subsequent ionisation energies and their relationship to electron shells

The second and third ionisation energies of an element X are the **enthalpy changes** for the reactions:

$$X^+(g) \rightarrow X^{2+}(g) + e^-$$

$$X^{2+}(g) \rightarrow X^{3+}(g) + e^-$$

Examiners' Notes

This variation across Period 3 is regarded as evidence for the existence of electronic sub-levels.

Successive ionisation energies can provide a very useful guide to the number of electrons in the outside shell (electron energy level) of an element. For example, the successive ionisation energies for aluminium vary as Fig 7 shows.

Fig 7
Successive ionisation energies for aluminium

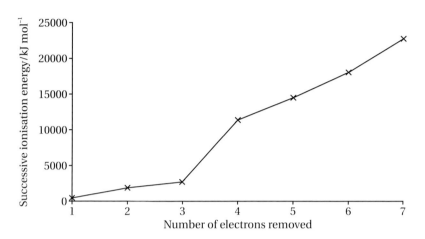

There is a big jump after removal of the third electron because the next electron must be removed from an inner shell. The graph in Fig 7 shows that aluminium has three electrons in its outside shell and is therefore in Group 3.

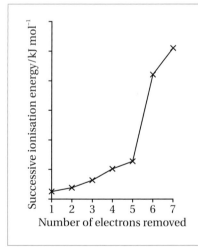

Example
In which group in the Periodic Table is this element to be found?

Answer
The large jump after the fifth electron shows that this element is in Group 5.

3.1.2 Amount of substance

Relative atomic mass and relative molecular mass

The isotope ^{12}C is the standard for relative mass:

Examiners' Notes

The average mass must be used to allow for the presence of isotopes.

$$\text{Relative atomic mass } (A_r) = \frac{\text{average mass per atom of an element}}{\frac{1}{12} \times \text{mass of one atom of } ^{12}C}$$

$$\text{Relative molecular mass } (M_r) = \frac{\text{average mass of a molecule}}{\frac{1}{12} \times \text{mass of one atom of } ^{12}C}$$

For compounds that are not molecules, relative formula mass is used.

$$\text{Relative formula mass } (M_r) = \frac{\text{average mass of an 'entity'}}{\frac{1}{12} \times \text{mass of one atom of } {}^{12}C}$$

Moles and the Avogadro constant (1)

The **Avogadro constant** is a quantity and is given the symbol L:

$$L = 6.022 \times 10^{23} \text{ particles mol}^{-1}$$

The **mole** is a quantity of particles:

1 mol is 6.022×10^{23} particles

1 mol of ^{12}C has a mass of precisely 12.000 g because ^{12}C is the standard.

1 mol of CH_4 molecules has a mass of approximately 16.0 g. It is calculated by adding up the individual values of the relative atomic masses:

$1 \times C = 12.0$

$4 \times H = 4 \times 1.0 = 4.0$

total mass $= 12.0 + 4.0 = 16.0$

This mass is approximate for two reasons:

- the relative atomic mass of ^1_1H is 1.0078
- carbon and hydrogen occur naturally as isotopic mixtures.

Different isotopes of carbon and hydrogen, such as ^{13}C and ^2H, occur naturally, so a few of the methane molecules have a mass which is greater than the mass of a $^{12}C^1H_4$ molecule.

A chemical equation usually implies quantities in moles. For example:

CH_4	+	$2O_2$	$\rightarrow$	CO_2	+	$2H_2O$
1 mol of methane molecules		2 mol of oxygen molecules		1 mol of carbon dioxide molecules		2 mol of water molecules

The **concentration** of a solution is a quantitative expression with units of mol dm^{-3}:

$$\text{concentration} = \frac{\text{number of moles of solute}}{\text{volume of solution in dm}^3}$$

A 1.0 mol dm^{-3} solution contains 1 mol of a substance which has been dissolved in enough water to make 1 dm^3 of solution. For example:

a 1.0 mol dm^{-3} solution of Na_2SO_4 contains:

$(23.0 \times 2) + 32.0 + (16.0 \times 4) = 142.0$ g of Na_2SO_4 in 1 dm^3 of solution

Three of the most useful methods for calculating the number of moles of a substance are as follows:

1 For a known mass of substance:

$$\text{number of moles} = \frac{\text{mass}}{M_r} = \frac{\text{mass}}{\text{mass of 1 mol}} = \frac{\text{mass in g}}{M_r \text{ expressed in g}}$$

Essential Notes

An 'entity' is a 'formula unit'.

Essential Notes

The symbol for the unit of the mole is mol.

Essential Notes

The mass of one atom of an element is very tiny. The mass of L atoms of an element is a recognisable number of grams.

Examiners' Notes

This degree of accuracy – to one decimal place – is sufficient for most chemical purposes.

Examiners' Notes

Problems with units? Think of a metre rule:

1 m = 10 dm = 100 cm

1 m^3 = 10^3 dm^3 = $(100)^3$ cm^3

= 10^6 cm^3

2 *For solutes in a solution, if the volume of the solution is known:*

number of moles of solute = volume of solution in dm^3 × concentration

$$= \frac{\text{volume of solution in } cm^3}{1000} \times \text{concentration}$$

Essential Notes

This equation is discussed in more depth in the next section.

3 *For gases:*

$$\text{number of moles} = \frac{pV}{RT}$$

Ideal gas equation

An **ideal gas** obeys the assumptions of the kinetic theory of gases. According to this theory, ideal gas particles (molecules or free atoms) are treated as hard spheres of negligible size which move with rapid random motion and experience no intermolecular forces.

The ideal gas equation is:

$$pV = nRT$$

Essential Notes

One Pascal (Pa) is one Newton per square metre ($N\ m^{-2}$)

p is the pressure of the gas in Pa

V is the volume of the gas in m^3

n is the number of moles of gaseous particles

R is the gas constant ($8.31\ J\ K^{-1}\ mol^{-1}$)

T is the temperature in kelvins (add 273 to the temperature in °C)

Essential Notes

100 kPa = 100 000 Pa

$200\ cm^3 = 200 \times 10^{-6}\ m^3$

25°C = 298 K

This equation can be used to find the number of moles (n) of a gaseous substance. For example, in $200\ cm^3$ of CH_4 at 25°C and 100 kPa the number of moles of methane is:

$$n = \frac{pV}{RT} = \frac{100\ 000 \times 200 \times 10^{-6}}{8.31 \times 298} = 0.008\ 08\ mol$$

Examiners' Notes

This is the basis of experiments to determine M_r by measuring the mass of a given volume of gas or vapour at a known temperature and pressure (gas syringe or bulb experiments).

If the mass and the number of moles of a sample are known, it is possible to calculate the relative molecular mass (M_r). The mass of the sample of methane above is 0.129 g. Hence:

$$M_r = \frac{\text{mass}}{\text{number of moles}} = \frac{0.129}{0.008\ 08} = 16.0$$

Empirical and molecular formulae

The **empirical formula** is the formula which represents the *simplest ratio* of atoms of each element in a compound.

The **molecular formula** gives the *actual number* of atoms of each element in a molecule (or the number of moles of each type of atom in 1 mol of the compound).

Calculation of empirical formulae
The empirical formula of a compound can be calculated from data which give the percentage composition by mass of each element in the compound.

Calculation of molecular formulae
The molecular formula can be deduced from the empirical formula if the relative molecular mass is known. A value for M_r can be determined as

shown using the ideal gas equation or from a mass spectrum. If a compound with empirical formula CH_2O has $M_r = 180$, the molecular formula can be calculated as shown at the end of the example below.

Example

A compound containing carbon, hydrogen and oxygen gave, after elemental analysis, the following percentages by mass:
C 40% and H 6.7%.

The percentage of oxygen is often calculated by difference. In this case, the percentage of oxygen = 100 − (40 + 6.7) = 53.3%.

The empirical formula can be calculated as follows.

Assume that there are 100 g of the compound, then the masses of the elements are:

   C 40 g; H 6.7 g; O 53.3 g

The number of moles of each element is calculated as follows:

$$\text{carbon: } \frac{\text{mass}}{A_r} = \frac{40}{12.0} = 3.3 \quad \text{hydrogen:} \frac{6.7}{1.0} = 6.7 \quad \text{oxygen: } \frac{53.3}{16.0} = 3.3$$

These numbers of moles can be expressed as a simple ratio by dividing through by the smallest number:

$$\text{ratio of moles of } C : H : O = 3.3 : 6.7 : 3.3$$

$$= \frac{3.3}{3.3} : \frac{6.7}{3.3} : \frac{3.3}{3.3}$$

$$= 1 : 2 : 1$$

Therefore the empirical formula is CH_2O

The empirical formula mass of CH_2O is 12.0 + 2.0 + 16.0 = 30.0

The ratio of M_r : empirical formula mass = 180 : 30.0 = 6 : 1

Therefore, in comparison with the empirical formula, the molecular formula must contain 6 times the number of atoms.

Therefore the molecular formula is $6 \times CH_2O = C_6H_{12}O_6$

Examiners' Notes

The molecular formula is always a whole number times the empirical formula.

Balanced equations and associated calculations

Balancing equations

Balanced equations must have the same number of atoms of each element on the left-hand side and on the right-hand side of the 'arrow'.

To balance equations, work through these steps.

1 Pick one element and see if the number of atoms of that element is equal on both sides of the arrow.

2 If the equation needs balancing, write the necessary number in front of the appropriate formula or symbol to make that element balance.

3 Move on to each new element and balance it in turn.

4 Check for fractions and multiply them out.

Examiners' Notes

For ionic equations the charges on the ions must also balance.

Thus $Fe^{3+} + Zn \rightarrow Fe + Zn^{2+}$

is not a balanced equation but

$2Fe^{3+} + 3Zn \rightarrow 2Fe + 3Zn^{2+}$

is balanced (6 positve charges on each side).

Example

Consider the unbalanced equation:

$$Al + NaOH \rightarrow Na_3AlO_3 + H_2$$

Taking each element in turn:

Al There is one atom (or 1 mol of atoms) on each side, so Al balances.

Na There is one Na on the left and three on the right – the equation is unbalanced.

Therefore use 3NaOH and the equation is now

$$Al + 3NaOH \rightarrow Na_3AlO_3 + H_2$$

O There are now three Os on each side, so O balances.

H There are three Hs on the left and two on the right. Using $\frac{3}{2}H_2$ on the right-hand side balances the equation:

$$Al + 3NaOH \rightarrow Na_3AlO_3 + \tfrac{3}{2}H_2$$

This equation is balanced, but it is better multiplied by 2 to avoid the fraction $\frac{3}{2}$:

$$2Al + 6NaOH \rightarrow 2Na_3AlO_3 + 3H_2$$

Calculating reacting masses and reacting volumes of gases

This skill is again best learned from examples.

Examiners' Notes

In calculations of this type the answer is usually expressed to three significant figures. It may be necessary to carry more accurate numbers through the calculation, but the answer should be rounded.

Example

Consider the following equation:

$$2HCl + Na_2SO_3 \rightarrow 2NaCl + H_2O + SO_2$$

If 1.00 g of Na_2SO_3 is reacted with an excess of HCl, calculate:

(i) the mass of NaCl produced by complete reaction

(ii) the volume of SO_2 gas produced at 30 °C and 100 kPa pressure.

Answer

Calculations like this almost always involve, as an intermediate step, working out numbers of moles. The answers can be deduced as follows:

(i) M_r for Na_2SO_3 is $(2 \times 23.0) + 32.0 + (3 \times 16.0) = 126.0$

$$\text{moles of } Na_2SO_3 \text{ used} = \frac{\text{mass}}{M_r} = \frac{1.00}{126.0} = 0.007\,94$$

From the equation, moles of NaCl = 2 × moles of Na_2SO_3

$$= 2 \times 0.007\,94$$
$$= 0.0159$$

M_r for NaCl $= 23.0 + 35.5 = 58.5$

mass of NaCl = moles × M_r

$$= 0.0159 \times 58.5 = 0.929 \text{ g}$$

(ii) From the equation, moles of SO_2 = moles of Na_2SO_3 = 0.007 94

Examiners' Notes

Remember

$1 \text{ m}^3 = 1 \times 10^6 \text{ cm}^3$

$1 \text{ cm}^3 = 1 \times 10^{-6} \text{ m}^3$

$$\text{volume } V = \frac{nRT}{p} = \frac{0.007\,94 \times 8.31 \times 298}{100\,000} = 1.97 \times 10^{-4} \text{ m}^3 = 197 \text{ cm}^3$$

Calculating concentrations and volumes of aqueous reagents

Work through this example of a typical problem.

Example

25.0 cm^3 of 0.102 mol dm^{-3} NaOH are exactly neutralised by a solution of 0.0830 mol dm^{-3} H$_2$SO$_4$:

$$H_2SO_4(aq) + 2NaOH(aq) \rightarrow Na_2SO_4(aq) + 2H_2O(l)$$

Calculate:

(i) the volume of sulfuric acid required for the neutralisation

(ii) the concentration of sodium sulfate in the resulting solution.

Answer

(i) moles of NaOH = volume (in dm^3) $\times$ concentration

$$= \frac{\text{volume (in cm}^3)}{1000} \times \text{concentration}$$

$$= \frac{25.0}{1000} \times 0.102$$

$$= 0.002\,55 \text{ mol}$$

From the equation:

moles of H$_2$SO$_4$ = $\frac{1}{2}$ $\times$ moles of NaOH

$$= \frac{0.002\,55}{2}$$

$$= 0.001\,275 \text{ mol}$$

number of moles of H$_2$SO$_4$ = volume in dm^3 $\times$ concentration

therefore volume of H$_2$SO$_4$(aq) = $\dfrac{\text{number of moles}}{\text{concentration}}$

$$= \frac{0.001275}{0.0830}$$

$$= 0.0154 \text{ dm}^3$$

$$= 15.4 \text{ cm}^3$$

(ii) moles of Na$_2$SO$_4$ produced = moles of H$_2$SO$_4$ used = 0.001\,275 mol

Ignoring the small amount of water produced in the reaction:

total volume of final solution = 25.0 + 15.4 = 40.4 cm^3

$$= 40.4 \times 10^{-3} \text{ dm}^3$$

concentration of Na$_2$SO$_4$(aq) = $\dfrac{\text{number of moles}}{\text{volume in dm}^3}$

$$= \frac{0.001\,275}{40.4 \times 10^{-3}} = 0.0316 \text{ mol dm}^{-3}$$

Examiners' Notes

The general way to progress through calculations like this is

- calculate the moles of known substance
- use the equation for the reaction and the moles of known substance to state the moles of unknown substance
- proceed to the answer.

Examiners' Notes

Remember

concentration

$$= \frac{\text{moles of solute}}{\text{volume of solution in dm}^3}$$

Also 1 dm^3 = 1×10^3 cm^3

$\quad\quad$ 1 cm^3 = 1×10^{-3} dm^3

Percentage atom economy

The **percentage atom economy** is a measure of how much of a desired product in a reaction is formed from the reactants. It is a theoretical quantity calculated from a balanced equation.

$$\text{percentage atom economy} = \frac{\text{mass of desired product}}{\text{total mass of reactants}} \times 100$$

Example

Consider the following equation for the production of dichloromethane (CH_2Cl_2):

$$CH_4 + 2Cl_2 \rightarrow CH_2Cl_2 + 2HCl$$

$$\text{percentage atom economy} = \frac{\text{mass of one mole of } CH_2Cl_2 \times 100}{(\text{mass of one mole of } CH_4 + \text{mass of two moles of chlorine})}$$

$$= \frac{85.0 \times 100}{(16.0 + 142.0)} = 53.8$$

This answer shows that $(100 - 53.8) = 46.2\%$ of the mass of reactants is converted into a co-product other than the desired product.

Percentage yield

Percentage yield is a practical measure of the efficiency of a reaction. It takes into account reactions that do not go to completion. It can only be calculated from experimental data.

$$\text{percentage yield} = \frac{\text{actual mass of product}}{\text{maximum theoretical mass of product}} \times 100$$

Example

Consider the following equation for the production of dichloromethane (CH_2Cl_2):

$$CH_4 + 2Cl_2 \rightarrow CH_2Cl_2 + 2HCl$$

In an experiment, 21.3 g of CH_2Cl_2 were produced when 8.0 g of methane were reacted with an excess of chlorine.

$$\text{number of moles of methane} = \frac{8.0}{16.0} = 0.50$$

Maximum number of moles of CH_2Cl_2 that can be formed from 0.50 mol of $CH_4 = 0.50$ mol
Maximum mass of CH_2Cl_2 that can be formed

$$= \text{number of moles} \times M_r = 0.50 \times 85.0 = 42.5 \text{ g}$$

Actual mass of CH_2Cl_2 formed = 21.3 g

$$\text{yield} = \frac{\text{actual mass of } CH_2Cl_2 \times 100}{\text{maximum theoretical mass of product}}$$

$$= \frac{21.3}{42.5} \times 100 = 50.1\%$$

This answer suggests that the reaction did not go to completion or that some of the methane was converted into by-products (or a combination of the two).

3.1.3 Bonding

Nature of ionic, covalent and metallic bonds

Ionic bonding

Positive ions are formed when atoms lose electrons:

$$Li\ (1s^2 2s^1) \rightarrow Li^+\ (1s^2) + e^-$$

Negative ions are formed when atoms gain electrons:

$$O\ (1s^2\,2s^2\,2p^4) + 2e^- \rightarrow O^{2-}\ (1s^2\,2s^2\,2p^6)$$

Compounds which contain ionic bonds are solids at room temperature. In solids, **ionic bonds** never exist in isolation. They form part of a **giant ionic lattice** where each positive ion is attracted by negative ions which surround the positive ion in a regular array. For example, the structure of NaCl in two dimensions is as shown in Fig 8. The positive ions are electrostatically attracted to the negative ions.

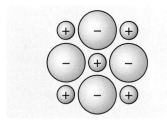

Ionic compounds conduct electricity when molten or in aqueous solution. The ions are fixed in position in the solid phase, but in the liquid phase, or in solution, they are free to move and carry the current.

Covalent bonding

Unlike ionic bonds, **covalent bonds** can exist in isolation in single molecules. In a covalent bond two atoms *share* a *pair* of electrons (•×) as shown in Fig 9.

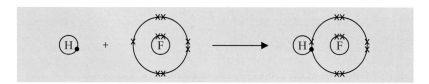

The electron pair creates a 'bond' between the two atoms because it attracts the nucleus of each atom and therefore resists the separation of the two atoms.

Co-ordinate bonding (dative covalency)

A **co-ordinate bond** is formed when both electrons in a shared electron pair originate from one atom (from a lone pair on the donor atom). As soon as it is formed, a co-ordinate bond is identical to a covalent bond (see Fig 10).

Fig 8
A slice through a three-dimensional ionic lattice of NaCl

Essential Notes

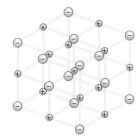

The sodium chloride lattice can also be drawn like this. The ions in this diagram are not drawn to be *space-filling*.

Fig 9
Formation of a hydrogen–fluorine covalent bond

Examiners' Notes

The shared pair of electrons in a covalent bond is usually represented by a line like this:

H—F

Fig 10
Co-ordinate bond formation

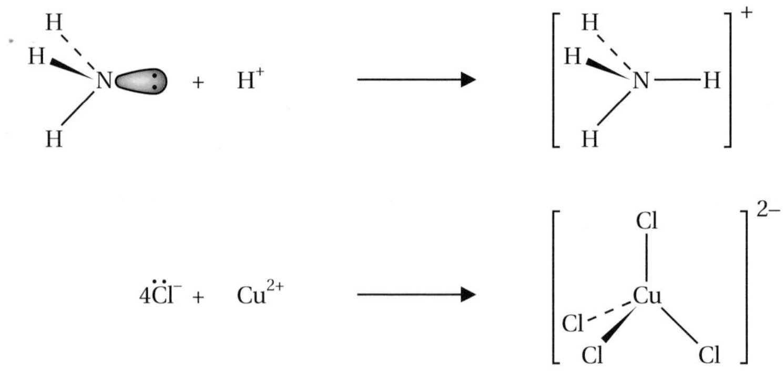

Essential Notes

Note that both of these ions have a tetrahedral shape, but are viewed from different angles.

The wedge represents a covalent bond coming out in front of the plane of the paper, and the dashed line a covalent bond going behind the plane of the paper.

represents a lone, non-bonding pair of electrons.

Metallic bonding

Metallic bonds in solids do not exist in isolation. They form part of a **giant metallic lattice** which consists of close-packed metal ions surrounded by delocalised electrons, which are free to move through the lattice. Fig 11 shows a metallic lattice in two dimensions.

Fig 11
A slice through a three-dimensional metallic lattice. The positive metal ions (cations) are held together by delocalised electrons (not shown)

Essential Notes

Delocalised electrons occupy an orbital which spreads across all the atoms that make up a metal crystal.

Metals usually have high melting and boiling points, because a large amount of energy must be supplied in order to remove a metal atom from the attraction of the delocalised electrons.

Bond polarity

Electronegativity

Electronegativity is the power of an atom to attract the electrons in a covalent bond. It can be calculated by various means and is usually given a number ranging from 0.7 to 4.0. Small atoms with a large number of protons in the nucleus attract bonding electrons most strongly. Therefore electronegativity increases from left to right across a period in the Periodic Table, and from the bottom to the top of a group (Table 5).

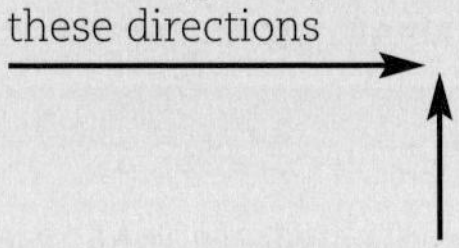

Table 5
Electronegativity values

H							He
2.1							
Li	Be	B	C	N	O	F	Ne
1.0	1.5	2.0	2.5	3.0	3.5	4.0	
Na	Mg	Al	Si	P	S	Cl	Ar
0.9	1.2	1.5	1.8	2.1	2.5	3.0	
						Br	Kr
						2.8	

Polar covalent bonds

When a covalent bond exists between atoms of differing electronegativity, the shared pair of electrons is displaced towards the more electronegative atom:

$$\overset{\delta+ \quad \delta-}{A-B} \quad \text{B is more electronegative than A}$$

The displacement of electron density makes the less electronegative atom slightly electron–deficient (hence δ+), while the more electronegative atom has a slight excess of electron density (hence δ-). This charge separation creates an electric 'dipole' and the molecule is described as **polar**. Two examples of molecules with polar bonds are shown in Fig 12.

The polarity of a bond can be measured in a unit called the debye. Its magnitude depends on the difference in electronegativity between elements (shown in Table 6).

Molecule	Electronegativity difference	Dipole/debye
HCl	0.9	1.03
HBr	0.7	0.78
HI	0.4	0.38

Forces acting between molecules

Covalent molecules are attracted to each other by intermolecular forces. The three types of intermolecular force are:

van der Waals'   permanent   hydrogen bonding
(temporary dipole–   dipole–dipole
induced dipole)

weakest   ⟶   strongest

This order of strength is true only for small molecules.

All species, even noble gas atoms, are attracted to each other by van der Waals' forces.

Polar molecules contain atoms with different electronegativities and, in addition to attraction by van der Waals' forces, these molecules attract each other by permanent dipole–dipole forces.

Molecules which contain hydrogen covalently bonded to a nitrogen, oxygen or fluorine atom are attracted to each other by hydrogen bonding. They are also attracted to each other by permanent dipole–dipole forces and van der Waal's forces.

Van der Waals' forces

Van der Waals' forces are *temporary dipole–induced dipole attractions*. At any instant in time, the electron distribution in a non-polar covalent

Examiners' Notes

$$\overset{\delta+ \quad \delta-}{A\blacktriangleright B}$$

This diagram shows how the electron pair in a polar bond is displaced towards the more electronegative atom.

Examiners' Notes

Note that it is *incorrect* to represent the polar hydrogen chloride molecule with full charges like this:

$$\overset{+ \quad -}{H-Cl}$$

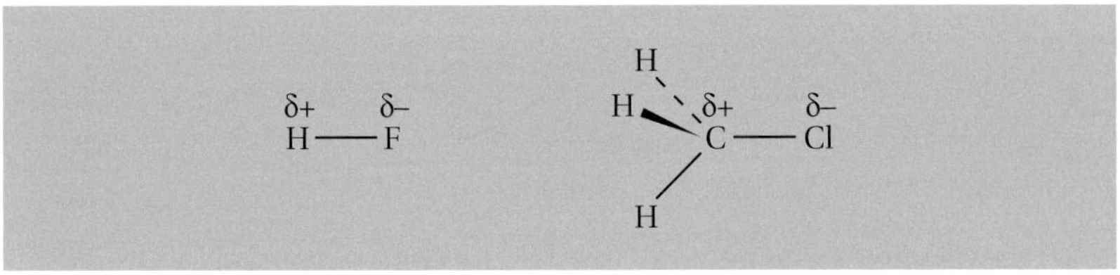

Fig 12
Polar molecules

Table 6
Polar molecules

Examiners' Notes

In some molecules, e.g. CO_2 and CCl_4, the bond polarities cancel so there is no overall polarity.

Essential Notes

In larger molecules van der Waals' forces are usually stronger than permanent dipole–dipole interactions.

molecule may be asymmetrical, owing to the fluctuating movement of electrons. This leads to a temporary dipole which induces an opposite dipole on an adjacent molecule. The second molecule is therefore attracted to the first molecule. The magnitude of van der Waals' forces increases with the size of molecules and also depends upon their shape. Branched-chain hydrocarbons have weaker intermolecular forces than straight-chain molecules because they are less polarisable.

Fig 13 helps to illustrate these effects. The ellipses represent the boundaries of the electrons in the molecules. The $\delta+$ and $\delta-$ charges shown are temporary and fluctuate around the molecules with time.

Examiners' Notes

For similar molecules the magnitude of the van der Waals' forces increases with relative molecular mass.

Fig 13
Van der Waals' forces in alkanes

Examiners' Notes

2,2-Dimethylpropane and pentane have the same formula (C_5H_{12}) and the same relative molecular mass, but the molecules of the branched-chain alkane, owing, to their more spherical shape, cannot pack together as closely and therefore the induced dipoles are weaker.

Essential Notes

T_b is the boiling point or boiling temperature.

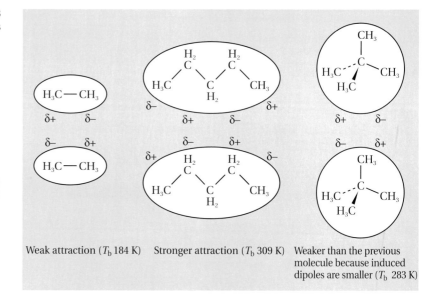

Weak attraction (T_b 184 K)   Stronger attraction (T_b 309 K)   Weaker than the previous molecule because induced dipoles are smaller (T_b 283 K)

Permanent dipole–dipole forces
Molecules with permanent dipoles attract each other as shown in Fig 14.

Fig 14
Dipole–dipole attractions

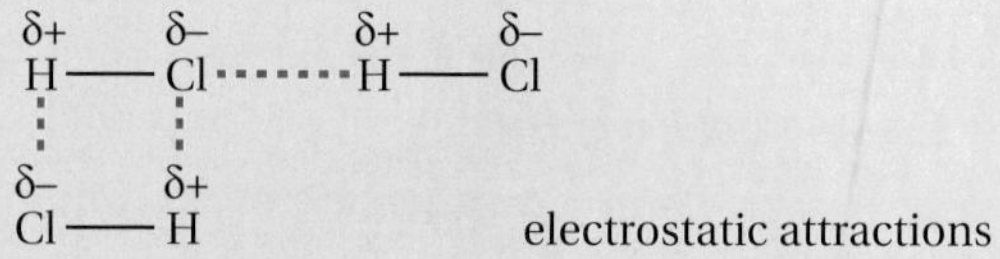

$$\delta+ \quad \delta- \qquad \delta+ \quad \delta-$$
$$H \!-\! Cl \cdots\cdots H \!-\! Cl$$
$$\delta- \quad \delta+$$
$$Cl \!-\! H \qquad\qquad \text{electrostatic attractions}$$

Hydrogen bonding
Hydrogen bonding is the name given to the strongest type of intermolecular force between neutral molecules. It is a special case of a dipole–dipole force that exists between a lone pair of electrons on a N, O or F atom and a hydrogen atom that has a strong partial charge ($\delta+$), because it is attached to an atom with a large electronegativity (N, O or F). The electronegative atom pulls electrons away from the hydrogen so that, on the opposite side to the bond, the hydrogen appears almost like an unshielded proton. Two examples of hydrogen bonding are shown in Fig 15.

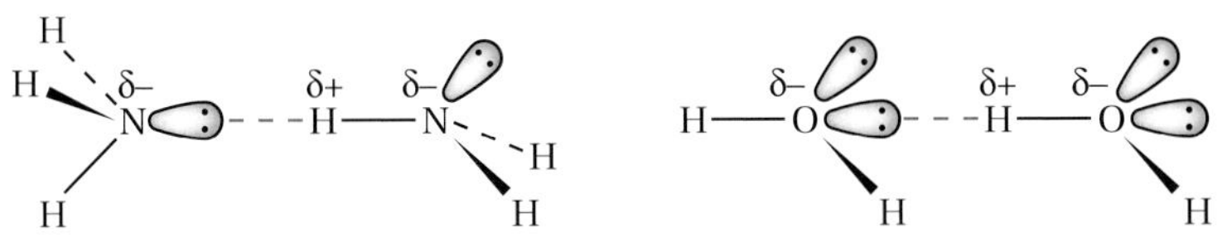

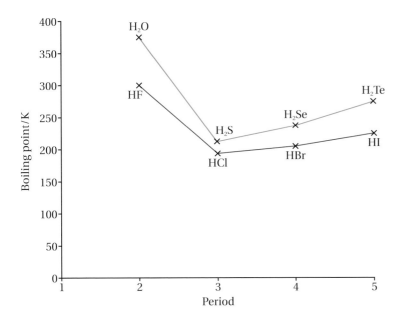

Fig 15
Hydrogen bonding

Other examples of molecules which hydrogen-bond to each other are HF, CH_3CH_2OH and CH_3COOH. These substances all have relatively high boiling points due to the hydrogen bonding.

The nucleus of a hydrogen-bonded hydrogen atom is always in line with the nuclei of the two electronegative atoms on either side. Hydrogen bonds are much weaker than covalent bonds – typically between 5% and 10% of the strength of a covalent bond. Nevertheless, this intermolecular force is strong enough to cause unusually high boiling points for some compounds (Fig 16).

Fig 16
Boiling points of Group 6 and Group 7 hydrides

The boiling points of hydrides generally increase down a group in the Periodic Table. The boiling points of HF and H_2O go against this trend, being higher than expected owing to hydrogen bonding.

Hydrogen bonding is also important because it influences the structures of some solids, such as the shapes of some proteins and the structure of ice.

In ice, hydrogen bonding holds the water molecules together in a three-dimensional array that occupies more space than in liquid water. This explains why ice is less dense than water and therefore floats.

Figure 17 is a simplified representation of the arrangement of water molecules in ice. The non-bonding electron pairs on the oxygen atoms are not shown and one of the hydrogen bonds to each oxygen has been omitted. In ice, the ring of six water molecules is not planar.

Fig 17
A simplified representation of six water molecules in an ice crystal.

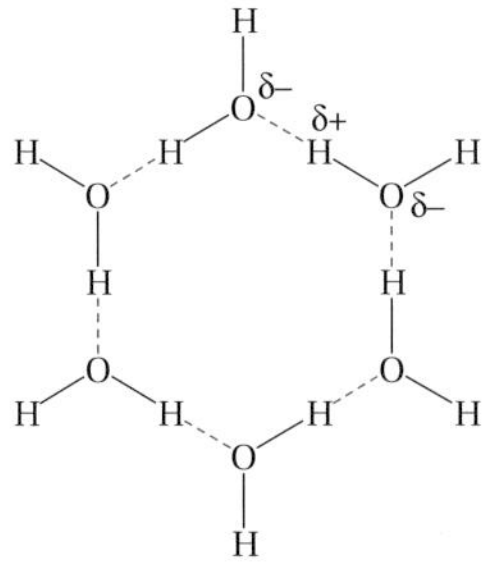

A more complete representation would show a three-dimensional structure, with each oxygen linked to four hydrogens using two covalent and two hydrogen bonds in a tetrahedral arrangement. Figure 18 shows in more detail a part of this three-dimensional structure.U

Fig 18
The three–dimensional nature of hydrogen bonding in ice or water (simplified)

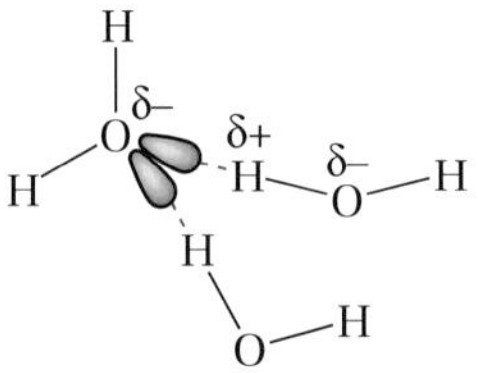

Hydrogen bonding is also responsible for some of the forces that hold protein molecules together and for protein molecules adopting the arrangement of a helix or a *'pleated sheet'* (see Fig 19).

Fig 19
Hydrogen bonding in protein molecules (simplified)

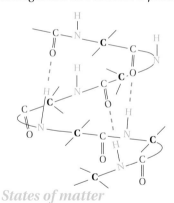

States of matter

Nature of gases, liquids and solids

Gases are made up of particles that are quite far apart and which move with rapid random motion. The size of the particles and any intermolecular forces can be ignored unless the particles are close together, at high pressure or at low temperature.

In liquids, the particles are in a state of order intermediate between that of a gas and that of a solid. At any instant in time the arrangement of particles resembles a somewhat disordered solid. Over a period of time the disordered regions allow all the particles in the liquid to move through the liquid. The particles are held together by forces similar to those in a solid.

In solids, the particles remain in fixed positions, about which they can vibrate. The forces which hold the particles together can be ionic attractions, covalent bonds, metallic bonds, hydrogen bonds, dipole–dipole forces or van der Waals' forces.

Essential Notes

The separation of particles in liquids is usually only about 10% more than in solids. In gases, separations are much larger.

Heat energy is required to change a solid into a liquid at its melting point. The energy is used to *loosen* the forces which hold the particles together. This heat energy is called the **enthalpy of fusion**.

More energy is needed to change *phase* from a liquid into a gas than to change from a solid into a liquid. The energy is used to *overcome* the forces which hold the particles together so that the particles can be completely separated. This heat energy is called the **enthalpy of vaporisation**.

Types of crystal

A solid with a regular shape which contains particles organised in a regular structure is called a crystal. Crystals can be classified according to the type of bonding between particles.

Ionic crystals. In the ionic lattice formed by sodium chloride, each sodium ion has six chloride ions as nearest neighbours and each chloride ion is surrounded by six sodium ions (see Fig 20).

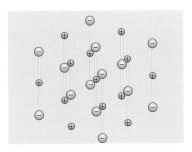

Ionic crystals usually have high melting points because the ions are held in position by strong electrostatic forces.

Ionic crystals are hard and brittle. They do not conduct electricity when solid, but when molten the ions are free to move and can carry a current.

Metallic crystals. In these crystals, the ions are usually packed together as closely as possible (see Fig 21). This means that each ion has six nearest neighbours in the same plane, three above and three below, making twelve nearest neighbours in total. The metallic bonds between ions are usually quite strong and most metals have high melting and boiling points.

Metals are malleable (can be hammered into shape) and ductile (can be drawn into wires) because the planes of ions can slide over each other. The bonding electrons are free to move between ions (the electrons are delocalised) leading to good electrical conductivity in the solid state. The delocalised electrons are also responsible for the ability of a metal to reflect light (metallic lustre).

Essential Notes

The term *phase* is most commonly used to describe transitions between solid, liquid and gasous states of matter.

Fig 20
The sodium chloride lattice

Fig 21
One plane of ions in a metallic crystal

Macromolecular (giant) crystals. The diamond crystal is very hard and has a high melting point, because all the carbon atoms are linked together by strong covalent bonds to form a giant crystal or **macromolecule** (see Fig 22).

Fig 22
Structures of the macromolecules diamond and graphite

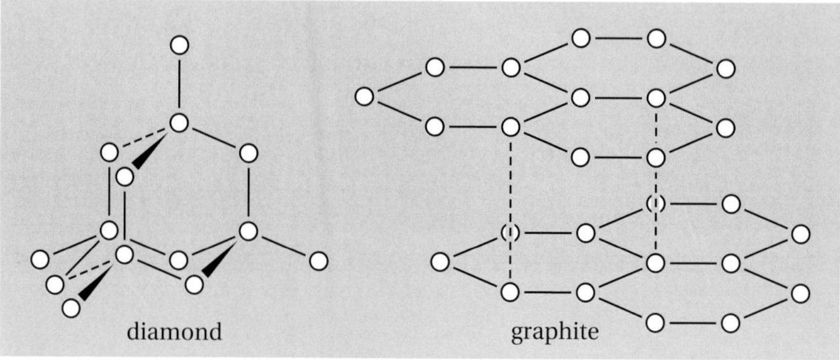

diamond   graphite

There are no covalent bonds between the layers in graphite. The dotted lines have been drawn to show the position of the second layer of carbon atoms relative to the first.

Graphite has a high melting point because all the atoms in each plane are linked by strong covalent bonds. The forces between the planes are weak, so the planes can slide over each other and, unlike most other macromolecules, graphite crystals are therefore soft. Exceptionally, for a macromolecule, graphite is able to conduct electricity because there are delocalised electrons above and below each plane of atoms. The delocalised electrons are free to move parallel to the planes.

Molecular crystals. The covalent molecules in molecular crystals are held together by one or more of the following interactions: weak van der Waals' forces, dipole–dipole forces or hydrogen bonding. In an iodine crystal the molecules are arranged in a regular array, but the forces between molecules are weak van der Waals' forces and so the crystal has a low melting point.

Properties of solids

The different types of crystal can be recognised by their physical properties as summarised in Table 7.

Examiners' Notes

Macromolecules melt at very high temperatures. Graphite is unique; most macromolecules are non-conductors under all conditions. However, some electrically-conducting polyethynes have been synthesised and used in rechargeable batteries and in electroluminescent devices.

Examiners' Notes

molecules in a crystal of iodine

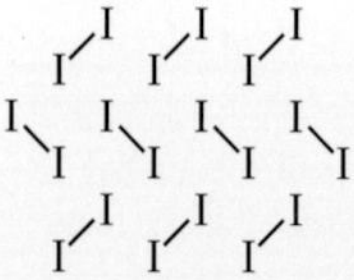

Molecular crystals like iodine are soft and break easily. They are non-conductors.

Table 7
Some physical properties of crystals

Type of crystal	T_m and T_b (relative values)	Electrical conductivity when solid	Electrical conductivity when molten	Solubility in water
ionic	high	non-conductor	good	variable but often good
macromolecular	very high	non-conductor (except graphite)	non-conductor	insoluble
molecular	low	non-conductor	non-conductor	variable
metallic	usually high	good	good	insoluble

Essential Notes

T_m is the melting point or melting temperature.

Shapes of simple molecules and ions in terms of electron-pair repulsion

The outer electrons of atoms in molecules are arranged in pairs. These electron pairs can be considered as 'clouds' of electron density which repel each other, so that they are as far apart as possible. This leads to the arrangements of electron pairs and the bond angles shown in Table 8.

Number of pairs of electrons	Arrangement	Angles	Name of shape
2 pairs		180°	linear
3 pairs		120°	trigonal planar
4 pairs		109.5°	tetrahedral
5 pairs		90°, 120°	trigonal bipyramidal
6 pairs		90°	octahedral

Table 8
Shapes of molecules

Examiners' Notes

Note: it is the repulsion between electron pairs which dictates the shape of a molecule or ion, *not* the repulsion between atoms.

The shapes of molecules and ions which contain only *single covalent bonds* between their atoms can therefore be predicted from the total number of electron pairs in the outside shell of the central atom. This number of electron pairs is calculated by taking into consideration:

- the number of outside-shell electrons originally in the central atom
- the number of additional shared electrons in covalent or co-ordinate bonds
- the loss or gain of additional electrons if the species is a positive or a negative ion.

The final shape is also modified if some of the electron pairs are lone (non-bonding) pairs. Lone pairs are more compact than bonding pairs so they repel each other and other pairs more strongly, leading to bond angles between bonding pairs which are *smaller* than those found in totally symmetrical shapes. These principles can be used to predict different shapes, as illustrated in Table 9.

Examiners' Notes

Lone pair–lone pair repulsions are stronger than lone pair–bonding pair repulsions. These in turn are stronger than bonding pair–bonding pair repulsions.

Table 9
Determination of the shapes
of molecules and ions

Molecule or ion	Outside shell electrons	Total number of electrons	Number of electron pairs	Shape
BF_3	3 from B +1 from each F	6	3	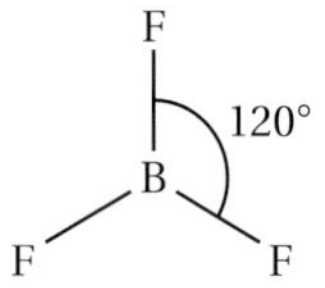 the three electron pairs repel equally
CH_4	4 from C +1 from each H	8	4	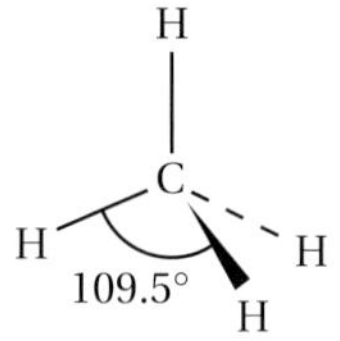
NH_3	5 from N +1 from each H	8	4	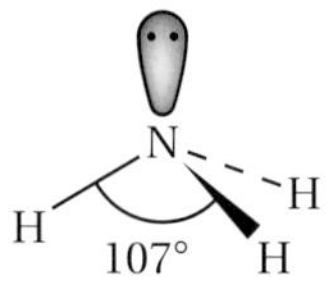 the single lone pair does not repel as strongly as the 2 lone pairs in H_2O
H_2O	6 from O +1 from each H	8	4	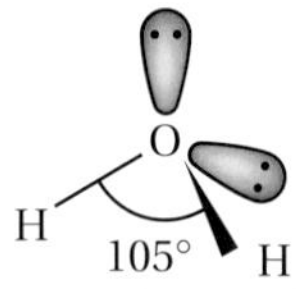 the lone pairs repel more strongly than the bonding pairs
PF_5	5 from P +1 from each F	10	5	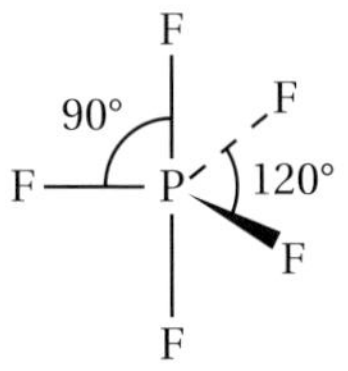
SF_6	6 from S +1 from each F	12	6	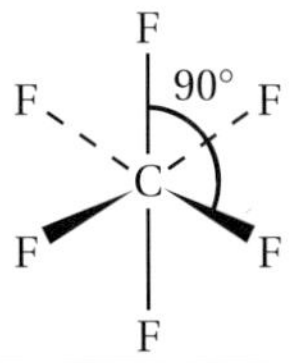
ClF_4^-	7 from Cl +1 from each F +1 negative ion	12	6	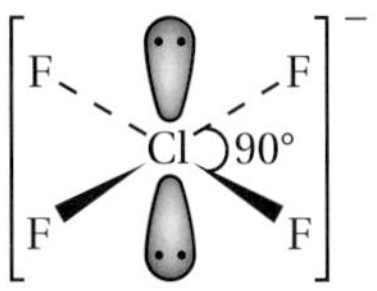 the lone pairs repel most, therefore they are as far apart as possible

Essential Notes

The bond angle in water is less than the tetrahedral angle.

Essential Notes

In this ion the electron pairs are arranged octahedrally. The shape of the ion is described as **square planar**.

3.1.4 Periodicity

Classification of elements in s, p and d blocks

Elements are classified in the Periodic Table as shown in Fig 23.

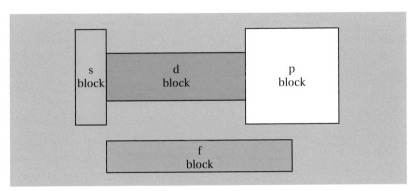

Fig 23
Classification of elements in the Periodic Table

Essential Notes

The letters s, p, d and f, which are used to describe electronic sub-levels (orbitals), originate from the description of lines in atomic emission spectra. The emission lines were described as **s**harp, **p**rincipal (the brightest lines), **d**iffuse and **f**aint (or fundamental).

In these blocks, the elements have their highest-energy electrons in s, p, d or f electronic sub-levels. For example:

- Li ($1s^2\,2s^1$) and Mg ($1s^2\,2s^2\,2p^6\,3s^2$) are s-block elements
- Cl ($1s^2\,2s^2\,2p^6\,3s^2\,3p^5$) is a p-block element
- Co ($1s^2\,2s^2\,2p^6\,3s^2\,3p^5\,4s^2\,3d^7$) is a d-block element.

Properties of the elements of Period 3 (Na–Ar) to illustrate periodic trends

Atomic radius

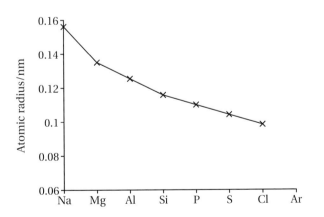

Fig 24
Atomic radii of the Period 3 elements

Essential Notes

The atomic radius of these elements is measured in suitable compounds of the element. Argon forms no compounds and therefore it is not possible to measure its atomic radius in a way which can be compared with the other elements.

The atomic radii decrease because, across the period, the nuclear charge increases and the outer electrons are attracted more strongly. They are therefore drawn closer to the nucleus, without any significant increase in shielding of the nuclear charge by the added electrons (see Fig 24).

First ionisation energy
This trend was discussed in section 3.1.1.

Melting and boiling points

Fig 25
Melting and boiling points of the Period 3 elements

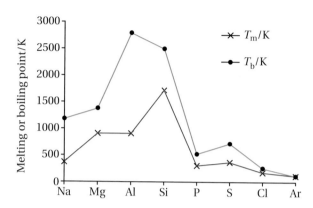

Essential Notes

Argon has a very low melting and boiling point because it exists as individual atoms. The atoms are not very polarisable and therefore the van der Waals' forces are very weak.

The variation in the melting and boiling points (Fig 25) is linked to the bond strength and the structure of the elements.

From sodium to aluminium the elements are metals. The melting and boiling points increase because, from sodium to aluminium, the atoms are smaller and have an increasing nuclear charge. Therefore, the strength of metallic bonding increases.

Silicon has high melting and boiling points because it is macromolecular, with a diamond structure, and strong covalent bonds link all the atoms in three dimensions. A great deal of energy is required to break these bonds.

Phosphorus, sulfur and chlorine are all molecular substances. The melting point (Table 10) of each is determined by the strength of van der Waals' forces between molecules which, in turn, are determined by the sizes of the molecules. Each of these elements has a low melting point because the van der Waals' forces are weak and easily broken.

Table 10
Melting and boiling points of some Period 3 elements

Molecular formula	P_4	S_8	Cl_2
Melting point/K	317	392	172
Boiling point/K	553	718	238

Essential Notes

Phosphorus and sulfur exist in different forms, but the molecular formulae shown are the simplest and most common.

The sulfur molecule is the biggest and most polarisable, so that sulfur has a melting point which is higher than that of phosphorus or chlorine.

3.1.5 Introduction to organic chemistry

Organic chemistry is the study of the many millions of covalent compounds of the element carbon. These compounds constitute an enormous variety of materials, ranging from molecules in living systems to synthetic materials made from petroleum, such as drugs, medicines and plastics. In sections 3.1.5 and 3.1.6 we consider mainly the chemistry of molecules derived from the hydrocarbons (compounds containing only C and H atoms) present in petroleum.

Some terms

Whenever a new compound is studied, it is first analysed to determine the percentage composition by mass of each of the elements present. From the data obtained, the **empirical formula** of the substance can be derived (see section 3.1.2).

Definition
*The **empirical formula** gives the simplest ratio of atoms of each element in a compound.*

Although the empirical formula of a compound X, CH_2O, gives the simplest ratio of atoms, this ratio can be found in many different molecules. From the empirical formula we can determine the **molecular formula**.

Definition
*The **molecular formula** gives the actual number of atoms of each element present in a molecule.*

The molecular formula must be a multiple of the empirical formula, i.e. $(CH_2O)_n$ in this example. In order to discover the value of n in the formula $(CH_2O)_n$, we need to know the relative molecular mass of compound X. The mass of the empirical formula CH_2O is 30. Thus, if the relative molecular mass of X is found to be 60, then the value of n is 2 and the molecular formula is $(CH_2O)_2$, which is more usually written as $C_2H_4O_2$.

This molecular formula, $C_2H_4O_2$, can represent several compounds in which the two atoms of carbon, four atoms of hydrogen and two atoms of oxygen are arranged differently. These different molecules are called **isomers**.

Definition
***Structural isomers** are compounds with the same molecular formula but different structures.*

The molecular formula for X, $C_2H_4O_2$, can represent several structural isomers. The structures of these isomers can be shown by displayed formulae or by structural formulae.

Definition
*A **displayed formula** shows all the bonds present in a molecule.*

Essential Notes

Isomerism is considered in detail later in this section and in *Collins Student Support Materials: Unit 4 – Kinetics, Equilibria and Organic Chemistry*, section 3.4.4.

Displayed formulae for two isomers of $C_2H_4O_2$ are shown below in Fig 26.

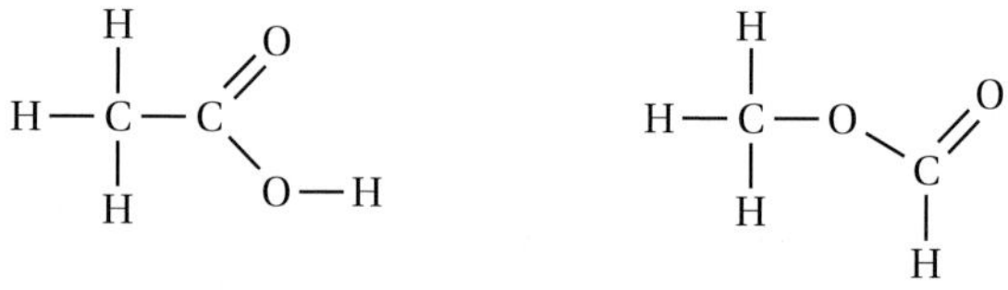

Fig 26
Two structural isomers of $C_2H_4O_2$ shown as displayed formulae

However, it is not necessary to show all of the bonds in a molecule to give a true picture of its structure, so it is simpler and more common to use a structural formula.

> **Definition**
> A **structural formula** shows the unique arrangement of atoms in a particular molecule in a simplified form, without showing all the bonds.

Structural formulae for the same two isomers of $C_2H_4O_2$ are shown below in Fig 27.

Fig 27
Two structural isomers of $C_2H_4O_2$ shown as structural formulae

These structural formulae do not show all the bonds present, but make it clear which isomer is which by displaying clearly which functional groups (see page 31) are present.

Representation of these two isomers either by displayed or structural formulae is an approximation since the molecules are three-dimensional, not planar as shown here. Displayed formulae can be cumbersome to draw so, particularly in equations, structural or simplified structural formulae are usually used, as in Equation 1.

$$CH_3COOH + CH_3CH_2OH \rightarrow CH_3COOCH_2CH_3 + H_2O \qquad \text{(Eqn 1)}$$

The organic product of the reaction in Equation 1 is more simply written as $CH_3COOCH_2CH_3$ rather than the displayed formula in Fig 28.

Molecular formulae, however, should not be used in equations as this could lead to confusion between structural isomers. Equation 1 is unambigous, whereas the compounds in Equation 2 could easily be misinterpreted.

$$C_2H_4O_2 + C_2H_6O \rightarrow C_4H_8O_2 + H_2O \qquad \text{(Eqn 2)}$$

To identify a particular compound from among the possible structural isomers, the chemical and/or physical properties of the compound need to be studied. Nowadays the traditional technique of elemental analysis has largely been superseded by instrumental methods such as infra-red spectroscopy and mass spectrometry (see *Collins Student Support Materials: Unit 2 – Chemistry in Action*, section 3.2.11) and also nuclear magnetic resonance spectroscopy (see *Collins Student Support Materials: Unit 4 – Kinetics, Equilibria and Organic Chemistry*, section 3.4.11).

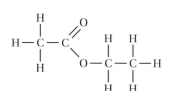

Fig 28
Displayed formula of $C_4H_8O_2$

Examiners' Notes

Structures must satisfy the rules of:

- 4 bonds to each carbon (tetravalent)
- 2 bonds to each oxygen (divalent) and
- 1 bond to each hydrogen (monovalent).

The organic compounds in this unit are almost all based on the series of hydrocarbons called alkanes (see section 3.1.6), in which one of the hydrogen atoms may be replaced by an atom or group of atoms called a **functional group**.

Definition
A *functional group* is an atom or group of atoms which, when present in different molecules, causes them to have similar chemical properties

The functional group is the reactive part of a molecule; the properties of the molecule are largely determined by the nature of the functional group.

A family of molecules which all contain the same functional group, but an increasing number of carbon atoms, is called an **homologous series**, and can be represented by a general formula.

The general formulae and functional groups for the homologous series of alkanes, alkenes and haloalkanes are shown in Table 11.

Homologous series	General formula	Name: prefix or suffix	Functional group	Example
alkanes	C_nH_{2n+2}	*suffix* -ane	none *	ethane C_2H_6
alkenes	C_nH_{2n}	*suffix* -ene	$\diagdown C = C \diagup$	ethene C_2H_4
haloalkanes	$C_nH_{2n+1}X$ X = a halogen	*prefix* halo-	—F or —Cl or —Br or —I	chloroethane CH_3CH_2Cl

Table 11
Homologous series, general formulae and functional groups

Essential Notes
Prefix means added before the rest of the name; *suffix* means the ending of the name.

* Alkanes, being the parent hydrocarbon, are not usually regarded as having a functional group

The general formula for alkenes, C_nH_{2n}, can also represent the homologous series of cyclic alkanes; for example, C_6H_{12} is the molecular formula of hexene and also of cyclohexane. The structure of cyclohexane is often simplified to a hexagon (see Fig 29).

All members of the same homologous series have similar chemical properties, since these properties are determined by the functional group present; their physical properties gradually change as the carbon chain gets longer. The boiling points of alkanes, for example, increase along the homologous series as the number of carbon atoms increases.

Fig 29
Two representations of cyclohexane

Examiners' Notes
In the molecule $C_nH_{2n+1}X$, C_nH_{2n+1} is called an alkyl group ('ane' in the name is replaced by 'yl'). Thus, CH_3 is called methyl. Alkyl groups are represented by the letter R.

Nomenclature: rules for naming organic compounds
Organic compounds are named according to the rules of the International Union of Pure and Applied Chemistry (IUPAC). These systematic or IUPAC names are based on the names of the parent alkanes. The first six alkanes are shown in Table 12.

Number of carbon atoms	1	2	3	4	5	6
Name	methane	ethane	propane	butane	pentane	hexane
Formula	CH_4	C_2H_6	C_3H_8	C_4H_{10}	C_5H_{12}	C_6H_{14}

Essential Notes
Each successive molecule in a homologous series contains an additional —CH_2— group.

Table 12
The first six alkanes

To assign the name of an alkane derivative, first look for the longest carbon chain in the skeleton; the number of carbons in this chain determines the stem of the name. Thus, if there are two carbon atoms in the longest chain, the stem name will be ethan-; if there are five carbon atoms, the stem name will be pentan-.

In many compounds the carbon skeleton is branched. The names of the side chains also depend on the number of carbon atoms in them, so that:

- a one-carbon branch is called methyl (CH_3-)
- a two-carbon branch is called ethyl (CH_3CH_2-)
- a three-carbon branch is called propyl ($CH_3CH_2CH_2-$)

The position of any branch on the chain must also be made clear. This is achieved by numbering the carbon atoms in the skeleton so as to keep the numbers used as low as possible when indicating the position of any branches. For example, the molecule in Fig 30 is called 2-methylpentane (numbering from the right) and not 4-methylpentane (numbering from the left).

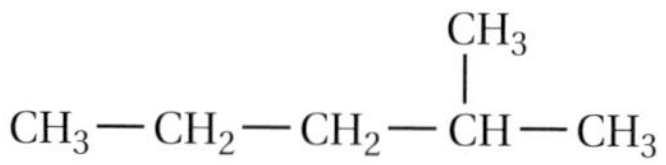

$$CH_3-CH_2-CH_2-\underset{\underset{CH_3}{|}}{CH}-CH_3$$

Note that, in these examples, the molecules are really three-dimensional with each carbon in the alkyl groups surrounded tetrahedrally by four bonds, with bond angles of approximately 109.5° (see Fig 31).

However, on paper it is usually simpler to represent a structure as if it had bond angles of 90° or 180°. For example, the three structures in Fig 32 all represent 3-methylpentane.

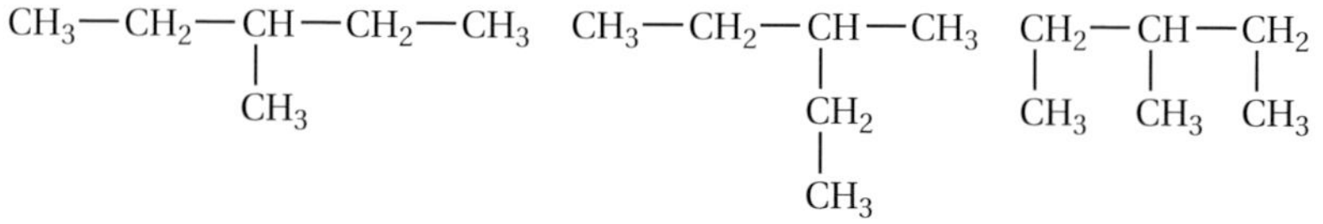

$$CH_3-CH_2-\underset{\underset{CH_3}{|}}{CH}-CH_2-CH_3 \quad CH_3-CH_2-\underset{\underset{\underset{\underset{CH_3}{|}}{CH_2}}{|}}{CH}-CH_3 \quad \underset{\underset{CH_3}{|}}{CH_2}-\underset{\underset{CH_3}{|}}{CH}-\underset{\underset{CH_3}{|}}{CH_2}$$

Naming molecules containing functional groups

- The *type* of functional group present is indicated by either a prefix or a suffix on the alkane stem (see Table 11).

- The *position* of the functional group is usually indicated by a number; e.g. 2-chloropropane (see Fig 33) has the chlorine atom on the second (middle) carbon atom.

- When two or more of a specific functional group are present, the *number* of substituents is shown by using the multipliers *di* for two, *tri* for three or *tetra* for four; for example dichloromethane, CH_2Cl_2, and tetrachloromethane, CCl_4.

- Numbers 1,2, etc. must also be used to show the position of each functional group. Commas are used between numbers and hyphens between numbers and letters; for example:

  CH_3CCl_3 is called 1,1,1-trichloroethane

  $CH_2ClCHCl_2$ is called 1,1,2-trichloroethane

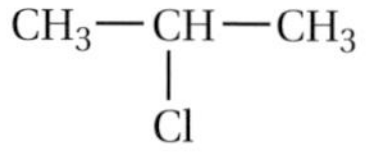

Examiners' Notes

$$CH_3-\underset{\underset{CH_3}{|}}{CH}-CH_3$$

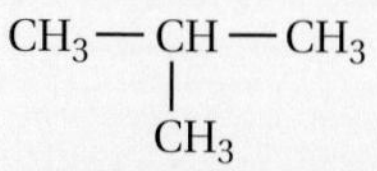

is called methylpropane as the longest chain has 3 carbon atoms (propane) with a one-carbon branch (methyl). No number is needed to show the postion of the methyl group as no other methylpropane is possible.

Fig 30
2-methylpentane

Fig 31
The tetrahedral arrangement of bonds around carbon

Fig 32
Different representations of 3-methylpentane

$$CH_3-\underset{\underset{Cl}{|}}{CH}-CH_3$$

Fig 33
The structure of 2-chloropropane

- If more than one type of functional group is present, the positions and names are listed as prefixes in alphabetical order, for example:

  $CH_3CHBrCH_2Cl$ is 2-bromo-1-chloropropane

- Multipliers are ignored when ordering substituents alphabetically; tribromo- will always come before dichloro-

- The suffix -ene for alkenes can be placed in front of other suffixes and is shortened to en if followed by a number, for example:

  $H_2C\!=\!CH\!-\!CH_2OH$ is prop-2-en-1-ol

Essential Notes

Where systematic names become complicated, trivial names are often used; for example, lindane is one of the three-dimensional isomers of 1,2,3,4,5,6-hexachlorocyclohexane.

Lindane is used as an insecticide in agriculture and also to treat lice.

Alternative representations for a lindane molecule:

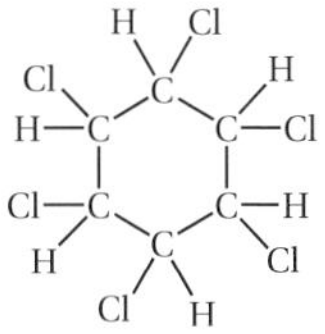

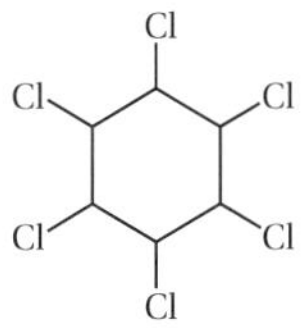

Drawing a structure from a given name

- Use the name to identify the number of carbon atoms in the longest chain
- Draw this carbon skeleton and number the carbon atoms
- Add any functional groups in the correct positions
- Add hydrogen atoms to make sure that every carbon atom has four bonds.

Example

The structure of 3-methylpent-2-ene can be deduced as follows:

pent- skeleton

$$C\!-\!C\!-\!C\!-\!C\!-\!C$$

pent-2-ene skeleton

$$\overset{1}{C}\!-\!\overset{2}{C}\!=\!\overset{3}{C}\!-\!\overset{4}{C}\!-\!\overset{5}{C}$$

3-methylpent-2-ene skeleton

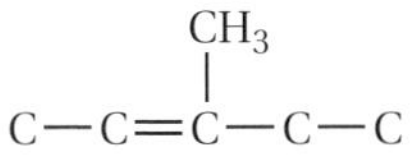

$$C\!-\!C\!=\!\underset{}{\overset{CH_3}{C}}\!-\!C\!-\!C$$

3-methylpent-2-ene complete

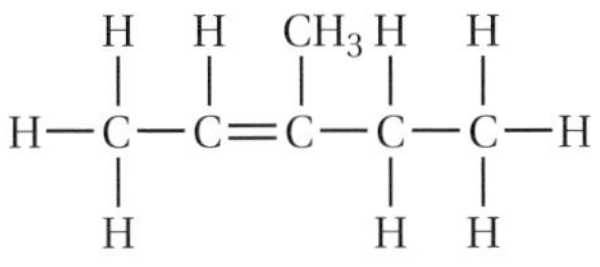

which can be written more simply as: $CH_3CH\!=\!C(CH_3)CH_2CH_3$

Examiners' Notes

When naming compounds, look for:

- the longest carbon chain
- functional group(s)
- the number of substituents
- where they are.

Isomerism

Isomerism occurs where molecules with the same molecular formula have their atoms arranged in different ways. Isomerism is divided into two main types, which are also themselves subdivided:

- **structural isomerism**
- **stereoisomerism** (see *Collins Student Support Materials: Unit 4 – Kinetics, Equilibria and Organic Chemistry*, section 3.4.4)

Structural isomerism

> **Definition**
>
> *Structural isomers are compounds with the same molecular formula, but with different structures.*

The different structures can arise in any of three different ways:

- chain isomerism
- position isomerism
- functional group isomerism.

Chain isomerism

Chain isomers occur when there are two or more ways of arranging the carbon skeleton of a molecule. For example, C_4H_{10} can be butane or 2-methylpropane, as shown in Fig 34.

Fig 34
The isomers of C_4H_{10}

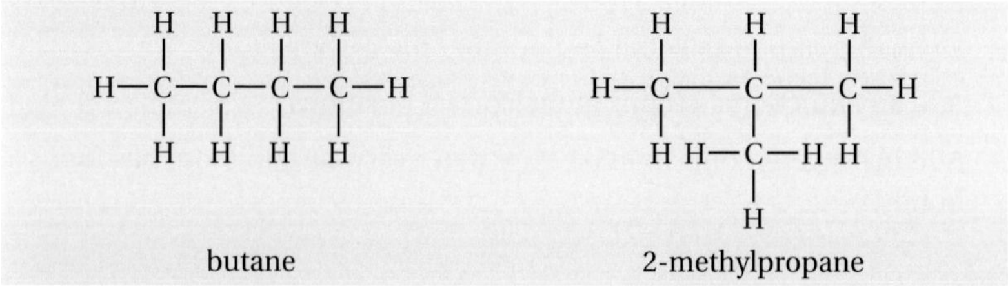

butane   2-methylpropane

Essential Notes

The number 2 is optional in 2-methylpropane (see page 32).

The three isomers of C_5H_{12} are pentane, 2-methylbutane and 2,2-dimethylpropane, as shown in Fig 35.

Fig 35
The isomers of
C_5H_{12}

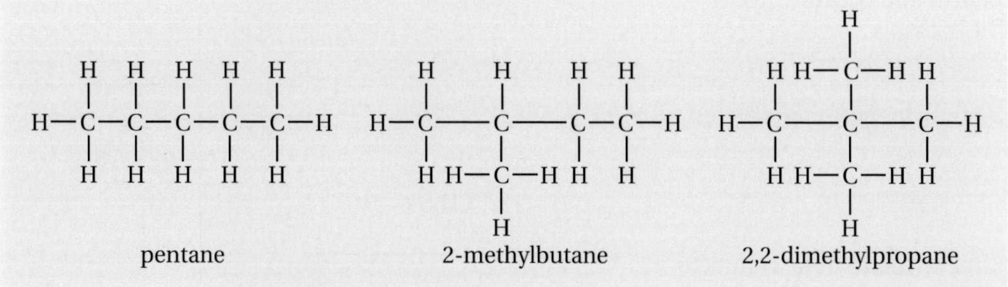

pentane   2-methylbutane   2,2-dimethylpropane

Essential Notes

The numbers 2 and 2,2 are optional (see page 32).

These isomers have similar chemical properties, but slightly different physical properties. Branched isomers have smaller volumes, weaker van der Waals' forces (see section 3.1.3) and therefore lower boiling points.

The number of structural isomers of alkanes rises steeply as the number of carbon atoms increases, as shown in Table 13.

Number of carbon atoms	Number of isomers
1	1
2	1
3	1
4	2
5	3
6	5
7	9
8	18
9	35
10	75
11	159
12	355
13	802
14	1,858
15	4,347
20	366,319
25	36,797,588
30	4,111,846,763
40	62,491,178,805,831

Table 13
The number of structural isomers of some alkanes

Position isomerism

Position isomers have the same carbon skeleton and the same functional group, but the functional group is joined at different places on the carbon skeleton. For example:

$CH_3CH_2CH_2Br$
1-bromopropane

$CH_3CHBrCH_3$
2-bromopropane

$CH_2 = CHCH_2CH_3$
but-1-ene

$CH_3CH = CHCH_3$
but-2-ene

Again, such isomers have similar chemistry because they have the same functional group, but the different positions can cause some differences in properties.

Functional group isomerism

Functional group isomers contain different functional groups and therefore have different chemical properties. For example, the molecular formula C_6H_{12} applies to cyclic alkanes, such as cyclohexane, and also to alkanes, such as hex-l-ene:

cyclohexane

$CH_3\ CH_2\ CH_2\ CH_2\ CH=CH_2$
hex-l-ene

The molecular formula C_3H_6O represents the aldehyde propanal and also the ketone propanone:

CH_3CH_2CHO
propanal

CH_3COCH_3
propanone

Examiners' Notes

These pairs of isomers can be distinguished by means of a simple chemical test (see *Collins Student Support Materials: Unit 2 – Chemistry in Action*, section 3.2.9 and section 3.2.10, respectively).

3.1.6 Alkanes

Fractional distillation of crude oil

Petroleum

Petroleum or crude oil is a complex mixture of hydrocarbons, mainly alkanes; it is derived from the remains of sea creatures and plants which sank to the bottom of the oceans millions of years ago. Subsequent deposits compressed this material and the high pressures and temperatures which developed – and also the absence of air – converted it into oil and gas.

Alkanes

Alkanes are the homologous series of **saturated hydrocarbons** with the general formula C_nH_{2n+2}. The first six alkanes are listed in Table 12. The lower alkanes are gases at room temperature; their boiling points increase with the number of carbon atoms because the strength of van der Waals' forces between the molecules increases. This increase in boiling points allows crude oil to be separated by fractional distillation (see below).

Alkanes contain only carbon–carbon and carbon–hydrogen bonds; these bonds are relatively strong and are non-polar. Consequently, alkanes are unreactive towards acids, alkalis, electrophiles and nucleophiles. In common with all hydrocarbons, however, they burn in air or oxygen with highly exothermic reactions; hence, they are important for use as fuels (see page 39).

Fractional distillation

The complex mixture of hydrocarbons in crude oil, mainly alkanes, is separated into less complicated mixtures, or fractions, by fractional distillation (primary distillation – so called as it is the first stage in the separation process).

A fractionating column or tower is the name given to the long vertical tube used in fractional distillation (see Fig 36). The crude oil is heated and the vapour/liquid mixture passed into the tower. The top of the tower is cooler than the bottom. The temperature gradient in the tower allows separation of the petroleum

Essential Notes

Saturated compounds contain only single bonds; unsaturated compounds contain one or more double or triple bonds.

Examiners' Notes

Electrophiles are electron-pair acceptors and seek electron-rich sites (see *Collins Student Support Materials: Unit 2 – Chemistry in Action*, section 3.2.9).

Nucleophiles are electron-pair donors and seek electron-deficient sites (see *Collins Student Support Materials: Unit 2 – Chemistry in Action*, section 3.2.8).

Fig 36
Fractionating column used to distill crude oil

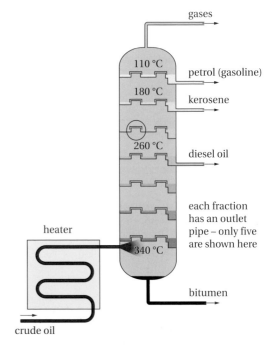

mixture into fractions depending on the boiling points of the hydrocarbons present. Only the most volatile components, those with low boiling points, reach the top; others condense in trays at different levels up the tower and are drawn off.

The residue from primary distillation still contains useful materials, such as lubricating oil and waxes; these boil above 350 °C at atmospheric pressure. At such high temperatures, some of the components in the residue decompose. To avoid this, the residue is further distilled under reduced pressure (vacuum distillation). Using this method, the remaining hydrocarbons can be distilled at a lower temperature where decompostion does not occur.

The major fractions and their uses are shown in Table 14.

Examiners' Notes

Fractional distillation is a *physical* process. Energy is needed only to separate molecules from each other, that is to overcome the van der Waals' forces.

Table 14
Fractions from crude oil

Name of fraction	Boiling range/°C (approx)	Uses	Length of carbon chain (approx)
LPG (liquefied petroleum gas)	up to 25	Calor Gas, Camping Gaz	1–4
petrol (gasoline)	40–100	petrol	4–12
naphtha	100–150	petrochemicals	7–14
kerosene (paraffin)	150–250	jet fuel, petrochemicals	11–15
gas oil (diesel)	220–350	central heating fuel, petrochemicals	15–19
mineral oil (lubricating oil)	over 350	lubricating oil, petrochemicals	20–30
fuel oil	over 400	fuel for ships and power stations	30–40
wax, grease	over 400	candles, grease for bearings, polish	40–50
bitumen	over 400	roofing, road surfacing	above 50

The composition of crude oil varies from one place to another. In general, however, the amount of each fraction produced by distillation does not match the demand (see Table 15).

Table 15
Supply and demand for oil fractions

Fraction	Approximate %	
	Crude oil	Demand
gases	2	4
petrol and naphtha	16	27
kerosene	13	8
gas oil	19	23
fuel oil and bitumen	50	38

A higher proportion of the high-value products (such as petrol) is used commercially than occurs naturally, while there is not enough demand for some of the heavier fractions. To solve this imbalance, larger alkane molecules are broken up into smaller molecules in a process called **cracking**.

Examiners' Notes

Cracking is a *chemical* process. Energy is needed to break C—C bonds.

Modification of alkanes by cracking

Cracking

Hydrocarbon cracking involves breaking carbon–carbon and carbon–hydrogen bonds. Two main processes are used: **thermal cracking** and **catalytic cracking**. In general, large alkanes are cracked to form smaller alkanes, alkenes and sometimes also hydrogen:

$$\text{high } M_r \text{ alkanes} \rightarrow \text{smaller } M_r \text{ alkanes} + \text{alkenes} (+ \text{ hydrogen})$$

These smaller alkanes are more in demand by the petrochemical industry and are therefore termed 'higher-value products'.

Ethene is another valuable product of cracking and can be used to make the plastic poly(ethene), commonly called *polythene*.

When cracked, molecules may break up in several different ways to form a mixture of products which can be separated by fractional distillation. For example, two possible fragmentations of the $C_{14}H_{30}$ molecule are:

$$C_{14}H_{30} \rightarrow C_7H_{16} + C_3H_6 + 2C_2H_4$$
$$C_{14}H_{30} \rightarrow C_{12}H_{24} + C_2H_4 + H_2$$

Thermal cracking

Thermal cracking results in the formation of a high proportion of alkenes. For example:

$$C_{14}H_{30} \rightarrow C_8H_{18} + 3C_2H_4$$

The energy required for bond breaking is provided by heat; the temperatures employed range from 400 °C to 900 °C at pressures of up to 7000 kPa. At the lower end of this temperature range, carbon chains break preferentially towards the centre of the carbon chain of the molecule. With increasing temperature, the cracking shifts towards the end of the chain, leading to a greater percentage of low M_r alkenes. In order to avoid decomposition into the constituent elements, the length of exposure to high temperatures (residence time) has to be short, of the order of one second.

Catalytic cracking

Catalytic cracking involves the use of zeolite catalysts (crystalline aluminosilicates), at a pressure slightly above atmospheric and a temperature of about 450 °C. By this means, large alkanes are converted mainly into branched alkanes, cycloalkanes and aromatic hydrocarbons. For example:

linear (unbranched) alkane — branched–chain isomer of octane — cyclohexane

Essential Notes

Aromatic compounds contain a benzene ring (see *Collins Student Support Materials: Unit 4 – Kinetics, Equilibria and Organic Chemistry*, section 3.4.6).

Examiners' Notes

Steam is used in the process to increase the yield of alkenes. By diluting the naphtha feedstock with steam, the formation of carbon is reduced and the transfer of heat to the reactants is improved.

Examiners' Notes

Bond enthalpy/kJ mol^{-1}

C—C 348

C—H 412

The C—C bonds are weaker and break more easily.

Essential Notes

When cracking is carried out in the presence of hydrogen (hydrocracking), the resulting mixture is free from impurities of sulfur (converted into hydrogen sulfide) and nitrogen (converted into ammonia) and also from alkenes (converted into alkanes).

The proportion of alkenes produced is small, so that catalytic cracking is primarily used for producing motor fuels. Branched-chain alkanes burn more smoothly than unbranched chains. In an engine, because of the pressures involved, the fuel–air mixture may ignite before the spark is produced, causing 'knocking'. This problem is prevented by using branched-chain alkanes.

Combustion of alkanes

In common with all hydrocarbons, alkanes burn in air or oxygen in very exothermic reactions and so are used as fuels. In the presence of a plentiful supply of oxygen, *complete combustion* of alkanes occurs to form carbon dioxide and water. For example:

$$CH_4 + 2O_2 \rightarrow CO_2 + 2H_2O \qquad \Delta H^{\ominus} = -890 \text{ kJ mol}^{-1}$$

$$C_4H_{10} + 6\tfrac{1}{2}O_2 \rightarrow 4CO_2 + 5H_2O \qquad \Delta H^{\ominus} = -2880 \text{ kJ mol}^{-1}$$

As the number of carbon atoms increases, more oxygen is required per mole of hydrocarbon for complete combustion, and more energy is released.

When insufficient oxygen is available, *incomplete combustion* occurs. Water is formed together with carbon monoxide or carbon. For example, if a bunsen burner is used with the air-hole closed, the flame is not blue but yellow and luminous, because of the carbon particles it contains. Any apparatus heated in a luminous flame becomes coated in black soot:

$$CH_4 + O_2 \rightarrow C + 2H_2O$$

Incomplete combustion forming carbon monoxide is, however, much more of a hazard. Badly maintained gas central heating boilers may produce carbon monoxide because of an inadequate supply of air, and can cause accidental death by carbon monoxide poisoning:

$$CH_4 + 1\tfrac{1}{2}O_2 \rightarrow CO + 2H_2O$$

Internal combustion engines

Carbon monoxide is also formed by the incomplete combustion of petrol vapour in a car engine:

$$C_8H_{18} + 8\tfrac{1}{2}O_2 \rightarrow 8CO + 9H_2O$$

Motor-car engines also produce other pollutants, notably oxides of nitrogen and unburned hydrocarbons. Oxides of nitrogen are formed when the air–petrol mixture is sparked and explodes. The temperature of burning petrol vapour can reach 2500 °C and this provides sufficient activation energy for nitrogen to react with oxygen to form nitrogen monoxide:

$$N_2 + O_2 \rightarrow 2NO$$

On cooling, nitrogen monoxide reacts easily with more oxygen to form nitrogen dioxide. With water and more oxygen, nitric acid is formed, which can lead to **acid rain**:

$$2NO + O_2 \rightarrow 2NO_2$$

$$4NO_2 + 2H_2O + O_2 \rightarrow 4HNO_3$$

Examiners' Notes

Complete combustion of hydrocarbons produces carbon dioxide and water.

Examiners' Notes

Incomplete combustion of hydrocarbons produces water and carbon or carbon monoxide.

Examiners' Notes

Cars with petrol engines produce carbon monoxide, but diesel engines produce only carbon.

Nitrogen dioxide also reacts with oxygen or hydrocarbons in the presence of sunlight to form an irritating photochemical smog.

Catalytic converters

These devices help to remove carbon monoxide, nitrogen oxides and hydrocarbons from car exhausts (see Fig 37). Converters contain a honeycomb of ceramic material onto which metals such as platinum, palladium and rhodium are spread in a thin layer. These metals catalyse reactions between the pollutants and help to remove up to 90% of the harmful gases. For example:

$$2CO + 2NO \rightarrow 2CO_2 + N_2$$

$$C_8H_{18} + 25NO \rightarrow 8CO_2 + 12\frac{1}{2}N_2 + 9H_2O$$

Overall, the pollutant gases – CO and NO_x and hydrocarbons – are replaced by CO_2, N_2 and H_2O, which are harmless.

Fig 37
The action of a catalytic converter

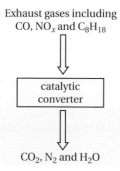

Exhaust gases including
CO, NO_x and C_8H_{18}

catalytic converter

CO_2, N_2 and H_2O

Combustion of sulfur-containing impurities

The alkanes and other hydrocarbons in petroleum fractions usually occur together with sulfur-containing impurities. When these hydrocarbons are burned, the impurities are also oxidised and form sulfur dioxide; for example:

$$CH_3SH + 3O_2 \rightarrow CO + 2H_2O + SO_2$$

Sulfur dioxide is a toxic gas and, being soluble in water, can cause acid rain by forming a solution of sulfurous acid, H_2SO_5. High in the atmosphere, ultra-violet radiation provides the energy for sulfur dioxide to react with oxygen to form sulfur trioxide. Sulfur trioxide is very soluble in water and forms sulfuric acid, which also occurs in acid rain.

A lot of sulfur dioxide is produced by the burning of fuels in power stations. However, this pollutant is not released into the atmosphere, but is removed from the gases passed up the chimney (flue) by a process called flue-gas desulfurisation.

Several alkaline substances can be used to remove the acidic sulfur dioxide. Some methods use calcium oxide (quicklime) which is easily obtained by heating calcium carbonate (limestone). The product of the reaction of calcium oxide and sulfur dioxide is calcium sulfite, $CaSO_3$.

$$CaO + SO_2 \rightarrow CaSO_3$$

Essential Notes

A suspension of limestone in water is also used to remove sulfur dioxide.

Calcium sulfite is easily oxidised and forms hydrated calcium sulfate (gypsum), $CaSO_4 \cdot 2H_2O$, which is used to make plasterboard for the building industry.

Greenhouse gases

Combustion of all fossil fuels, including alkanes, eventually produces carbon dioxide. This gas, together with water vapour, methane and ozone (the so-called **greenhouse gases**), is thought to contribute to global warming by absorbing infra-red radiation.

Ultra-violet and visible radiation from the sun is absorbed by the Earth and emitted at much longer wavelengths as infra-red radiation. This radiation is absorbed by some molecules in the atmosphere which trap the energy and prevent its escape. Not all gases absorb infra-red radiation, but those which do are called greenhouse gases.

Many governments have introduced measures to control or reduce the emision of carbon dioxide. Car manufacturers, for instance, must publish data about CO_2 emissions from their vehicles. Other fuels or methods of producing energy are also being considered as alternatives to the combustion of fossil fuels.

Essential Notes

The causes of global warming are not fully understood, the level of carbon dioxide in the atmosphere being only one of several factors involved.

Essential Notes

The absorption of infra-red radiation is considered in more detail in *Collins Student Support Materials: Unit 2 – Chemistry in Action*, section 3.2.11.

How Science Works

The introduction of the *How Science Works* component into the new A-level specifications has made formal an approach to the teaching of topics in science which many teachers have, in fact, already been using.

Irrespective of future careers, science students need to become proficient in dealing with the various issues included in *How Science Works* so as to achieve a level of scientific awareness. In order to gain an appreciation of how chemists, in particular, work (using the scientific method) it is necessary to understand and be able to apply the concepts, principles and theories of chemistry. The ways that chemical theories and laws are developed, together with the potential impact of new discoveries on society in general, should become clear to you as new concepts in the specification are explored.

Science starts with experimental observation and investigation, followed by verification (i.e. confirmation by others that the results are reliable). A theory or model is proposed to try to explain a set of observations, which may themselves have been accidental or planned as part of a series of experiments. During A-level chemistry courses, many different types of experiment will be carried out and evaluated.

Once an initial theory, or hypothesis, has been put forward to explain a set of results, further experiments are carried out to test the ability of this theory to make accurate predictions. An initial theory may need to be adapted to take into account fresh evidence. More observations and experimental results are produced and the cycle is continued until a firm theory can be established. It is very important that all experiments are carried out objectively, without any bias towards a desired result.

A-level Chemistry courses provide various opportunities for students to analyse verified experimental data as well as the chance to develop theories based on novel findings. In some instances, it will be recognised that there is insufficient experimental evidence for a firm theory to be accepted. In other cases, different experiments carried out by different people will produce contradictory results. Sometimes an apparently unusual result or observation, if verified, will be of great significance. There then follow opportunities to debate these issues and to understand how conflicting theories can be resolved by the accumulation of further evidence.

The concepts and principles dealt with under *How Science Works* will be assessed during the examination. The questions set will require only a knowledge and understanding of the topics included in the specification. In some instances, however, the ability to analyse and make deductions from unfamiliar information may be required. Typical examination questions are provided at the end of the Unit and aspects of *How Science Works* are highlighted.

Practice exam-style questions

1 **(a)** Complete the following table.

Name of fundamental particle	Relative mass	Relative charge
	5.45×10^{-4}	
		$+1$
		0

6 marks

(b) Give the meaning of the term *mass number*.

_____ 1 mark

(c) In terms of the numbers of fundamental particles, explain the difference between two isotopes of the same element.

_____ 2 marks

(d) Give the full chemical symbol for the isotope that has seven electrons and six neutrons in one atom.

_____ 2 marks

(e) Give the number of protons, neutrons and electrons in the ion $^{31}P^{3-}$

_____ 3 marks

(f) Give the full electronic configuration, including sub-shells, of the following species.

(i) Mg^{2+} _____

(ii) Cr _____

(iii) S^{2-} _____

(iv) Fe^{2+} _____ 4 marks

Total marks: 18

2   A diagram of a mass spectrometer is shown below.

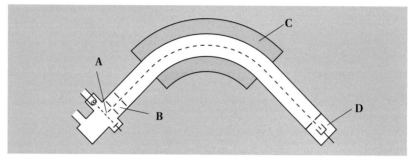

(a) Name the process that happens in region **A** and explain how it is achieved.

Name of process

Explanation

3 marks

(b) State the function of the part of the mass spectrometer labelled **B** and explain its action.

Function

Explanation

3 marks

(c) **C** is a powerful electromagnet. Explain the function of this electromagnet.

2 marks

(d) State the property that the detector **D** can measure and explain how the detector works.

Property measured

Explanation

3 marks

(e) Explain why the spectrometer is able to detect particles with different m/z values.

3 marks

Total marks: 14

3 A 2.00 g sample of an alloy of magnesium (alloyed with only one other metal, **M**) was reacted completely with 50.0 cm^3 (an excess) of a hydrochloric acid solution; 949 cm^3 of hydrogen gas were formed at 293 K and 101 kPa. The excess of hydrochloric acid was neutralised by reaction with exactly 21.3 cm^3 of 1.00 mol dm^{-3} sodium hydroxide solution. You may assume that metal M does not react with hydrochloric acid.

$$Mg(s) + 2HCl(aq) \rightarrow MgCl_2(aq) + H_2(g)$$

$$HCl(aq) + NaOH(aq) \rightarrow NaCl(aq) + H_2O(aq)$$

(a) State the ideal gas equation and use it to calculate the number of moles of hydrogen gas produced.

_____

_____

_____ 3 marks

(b) Use your answer to part (a) to calculate the mass of magnesium metal in the sample of magnesium alloy.

_____

_____ 2 marks

(c) Calculate the number of moles of NaOH used to neutralise the excess of HCl.

_____

_____

_____ 2 marks

(d) Use your answers to parts (a) and (c) to calculate the moles of HCl present in the original 50 cm^3 of solution, and hence calculate the concentration of HCl in this solution.

_____

_____

_____

_____ 4 marks

(e) Use your answer to part (b) to calculate the percentage by mass of metal **M** in the 2.00 g sample of alloy.

_____

_____ 2 marks

45

(f) **(i)** Explain why it is necessary to assume that the metal **M** does not react with hydrochloric acid.

_____

_____ 1 mark

(ii) You are provided with a pure sample of metal **M**. Describe a simple chemical test to show that metal **M** does not react with hydrochloric acid.

_____

_____ 1 mark

Total marks: 15

4   Consider the table below which contains information about the unknown substances **P**, **Q**, **R** and **S**.

Unknown	Melting point/K when solid	Electrical conductivity when liquid	Electrical conductivity
P	2600	poor	poor
Q	1810	good	good
R	1261	poor	good
S	463	poor	poor

For each of **P**, **Q**, **R** and **S**, predict their structures and their bonding, and account for the properties listed in the table.

_____

_____

_____

_____

_____

_____

_____

_____

_____

_____

_____

_____

_____

_____

Total marks: 15

5 **(a)** Explain how electron-pair repulsion theory can be used to predict the shape of, and bond angle in, an ammonia molecule.

_____

_____

_____

_____

_____

_____ 6 marks

(b) Draw diagrams to illustrate the shapes of the following molecules or ions and, on each diagram, write an approximate value for the bond angle(s) in that molecule or ion.

(i) H_2O **(ii)** $BeCl_2$

(iii) $[PCl_6]^-$ **(iv)** $[SF_5]^+$

9 marks

(c) Name and explain the origin of the forces of attraction that exist between H_2S molecules.

_____

_____

_____

_____

_____ 4 marks

Total marks: 19

6 Consider the following incomplete diagram.

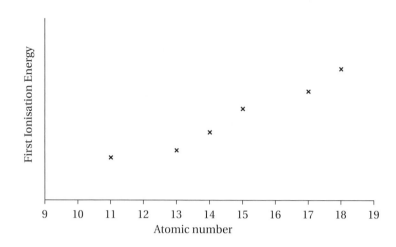

(a) Mark on the diagram, with labelled crosses, the first ionisation energies of neon, magnesium, sulfur and potassium.

_____4 marks

(b) For each of the elements in part (a), explain why you have marked your cross in that particular position.

_____

_____

_____

_____

_____

_____

_____

_____ 8 marks

Total marks: 12

7 Consider the following melting-point data.

Element	Sodium	Magnesium	Aluminium	Silicon	Phosphorus	Sulfur	Chlorine	Argon
Melting point/K	371	923	933	1680	317	392	172	84

Explain the following in terms of structure and bonding.

(a) Magnesium has a higher melting point than sodium.

_____

_____

_____ 3 marks

(b) Silicon has a higher melting point than aluminium.

_____

_____

_____

_____ 4 marks

(c) Phosphorus has a higher melting point than chlorine but a lower one than sulfur.

_____

_____

_____

_____ 4 marks

(d) Argon has a very low melting point.

_____

_____

_____

_____ 4 marks

Total marks: 15

8 **(a)** Analysis of a hydrocarbon shows that it has a relative molar mass of 56 and contains 85.7% carbon.

Calculate the empirical formula of the hydrocarbon and deduce its molecular formula.

Calculation _____

_____

_____

_____

Molecular formula _____ 4 marks

(b) Name the hydrocarbon shown below. Give its molecular formula and name the homologous series to which it belongs.

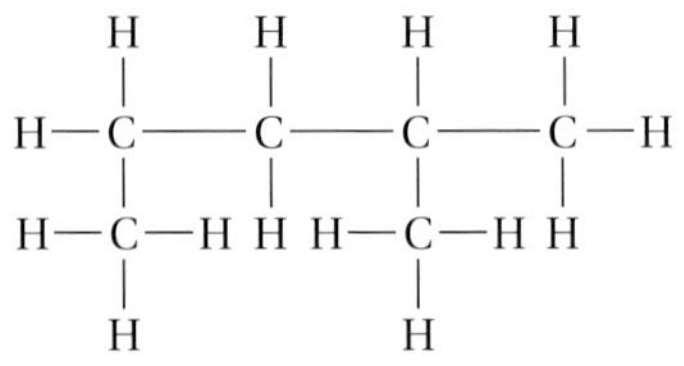

Name _____

Molecular formula _____

Homologous series _____ 3 marks

(c) Draw displayed formulae for the two structural isomers with molecular formula C_3H_7Cl. Name both isomers and state the type of structural isomerism they show.

Displayed formulae

Name of isomer 1 _____

Name of isomer 2 _____

Type of structural isomerism _____ 5 marks

Total marks: 12

9 (a) Write an equation for the complete combustion of the hydrocarbon C_8H_{18} that is used as a fuel.

_____ 2 marks

(b) An impure sample of C_8H_{18} contains a small amount of the compound CH_3SH. The compound CH_3SH burns in air to form carbon dioxide, water and sulfur dioxide.

(i) Write an equation for the complete combustion of CH_3SH.

_____

(ii) Explain, with the aid of an equation, how calcium oxide can be used to remove sulfur dioxide from exhaust gases produced when CH_3SH burns.

_____

_____

(iii) Suggest one environmental advantage of the removal of sulfur dioxide from exhaust gases and one environmental disadvantage of using calcium oxide for this process.

Advantage of SO_2 removal _____

Disadvantage of using CaO _____

_____ 5 marks

Total marks: 7

10 A hydrocarbon that is a member of the alkane homologous series has the molecular formula C_9H_{20}.

(a) Explain the meaning of the term *homologous series*.

_____

_____ 2 marks

(b) Give the molecular formulae for the preceding member and for the subsequent member of the same homologous series as C_9H_{20}.

Preceding member _____

Subsequent member _____ 2 marks

(c) The alkane C_9H_{20} can be cracked to form propene.

(i) State the type of cracking that would lead to formation of propene and give conditions suitable for this reaction.

Type of cracking _____

Conditions _____

(ii) A typical yield of propene in such a reaction is 30%. Give two reasons that could account for a yield of less than 100%.

Reason 1 _____

Reason 2 _____ 5 marks

(d) The alkane C_9H_{20} can be cracked to form propene and one other product.

(i) Write an equation for this reaction.

_____

(ii) Calculate the percentage atom economy for the production of propene in this reaction.

_____

_____

_____

(iii) Suggest how an industrial chemist might deal with this reaction to compensate for the low atom economy.

_____

_____ 5 marks

Total marks: 14

11 (a) Crude oil from different countries differs in its composition.

Crude oil from Saudi Arabia is called *light*. It is paler in colour and less viscous (i.e. more runny) than crude oil from Venezuela, which is called *heavy*.

(i) Suggest why *light* crude oil is less viscous.

_____

_____

(ii) Which type of crude oil is likely to be the more expensive and why?

_____

_____ 4 marks

(b) A student compared the combustion of three liquid alkanes: hexane (C_6H_{14}), nonane (C_9H_{20}) and dodecane ($C_{12}H_{26}$). She burned them separately in spirit burners and observed that the flame produced by hexane was the least smoky and that the flame produced by dodecane was the most smoky.

Write equations for the complete combustion of these alkanes and suggest why the smokiness of the flames varied.

_____

_____

_____

_____

_____

_____ 9 marks

(c) Write an equation for the thermal cracking of $C_{15}H_{32}$ to form octane and ethene in a 1:2 ratio, together with one other compound.

_____ 2 marks

(d) Oxides of nitrogen are found in the exhaust gases of cars.

Explain how the oxides of nitrogen are formed and how they are removed from the exhaust gases.

_____

_____

_____

_____

_____ 5 marks

(e) The gases released into the atmosphere from a coal-fired power station were tested by environmental inspectors and found to contain almost no sulfur dioxide. Explain how sulfur dioxide is formed in the power station and how it can be removed successfully.

_____

_____

_____ 3 marks

Total marks: 23

Answers, explanations, hints and tips

Question	Answer		Marks
1 (a)	electron (1)	relative charge –1 (1)	
	proton (1)	relative charge +1 (1)	
	neutron (1)	relative charge +1 (1)	6
1 (b)	number of protons + number of neutrons in the nucleus of an atom	(1)	1
1 (c)	same number of protons and electrons	(1)	
	different number of neutrons	(1)	2
1 (d)	$^{13}_{7}N$ 13/7 (1) N (1)		2
1 (e)	15 protons	(1)	
	16 neutrons	(1)	
	18 electrons	(1)	3
1 (f)	$1s^2 2s^2 2p^6$	(1)	
	$1s^2 2s^2 2p^6 3s^2 3p^6 4s^2 3d^4$ (or $3d^5 4s^1$)	(1)	
	$1s^2 2s^2 2p^6 3s^2 3p^6$	(1)	
	$1s^2 2s^2 2p^6 3s^2 3p^6 3d^6$	(1)	4
			Total 18
2 (a)	ionisation	(1)	
	gaseous particle hit by electron from electron gun	(1)	
	knocks out an electron from the particle to form a positive ion	(1)	3
2 (b)	to accelerate ions	(1)	
	electric field (or negative plate)	(1)	
	attracts positive ions	(1)	3
2 (c)	to deflect ions	(1)	
	so that they hit the detector	(1)	2
2 (d)	relative abundance of an ion	(1)	
	ion hits detector and accepts an electron	(1)	
	creates a current which is amplified and measured	(1)	3
2 (e)	magnetic (or electric) field strength can be altered	(1)	
	to change the amount of deflection	(1)	
	stronger magnetic field (or lower accelerating potential)		
	brings heavier ions to detector	(1)	3
			Total 14
3 (a)	$PV = nRT$	(1)	
	$n = PV/RT = 101000 \times 949 \times 10^{-6}/(8.31 \times 293)$	(1)	
	$= 0.0394$	(1)	3
3 (b)	moles Mg = 0.0394	(1)	
	mass = moles $\times$ 24.3 = 0.957	(1)	2
3 (c)	moles = 21.3 $\times$ 1/1000	(1)	
	$= 0.0213$	(1)	2

Question	Answer		Marks
3 (d)	moles of HCl reacted = 2 × 0.0394 = 0.0788	(1)	
	moles in excess = 0.0213	(1)	
	total = 0.1001	(1)	
	concentration = 0.1001 × (1000/50.0) = 2.00 mol dm^{-3}	(1)	4
3 (e)	mass of M = 2.00 – 0.957 = 1.043 g	(1)	
	% = 1.04 × 100/2.00 = 52.2%	(1)	2
3 (f) (i)	impossible to determine moles of Mg if M also reacts	(1)	1
3 (f) (ii)	weigh then place in HCl and allow to react	(1)	
	then wash, dry and re-weigh	(1)	2
			Total 16
4	P: macromolecular	(1)	
	covalent	(1)	
	lots of energy to break bonds	(1)	
	electrons immobile	(1)	
	Q: metallic	(1)	
	strong metal–metal bonds	(1)	
	delocalised mobile electrons carry a current	(1)	
	R: ionic lattice	(1)	
	strong forces of attraction between ions	(1)	
	ions immobile in solid, mobile in liquid	(1)	
	mobile ions carry current	(1)	
	S: molecular	(1)	
	covalent bonds in molecules	(1)	
	van der Waals' forces between molecules	(1)	
	electrons not mobile	(1)	15
			Total 15
5 (a)	8 electrons round N in outside shell	(1)	
	4 pairs	(1)	
	3 bonding, 1 non-bonding	(1)	
	electron pairs repel as far apart as possible	(1)	
	non-bonding pair repels more than bonding pairs	(1)	
	bond angle 107°	(1)	6
5 (b) (i)	bent or V-shaped	(1)	
	105°	(1)	2
5 (b) (ii)	linear	(1)	
	180°	(1)	2
5 (b) (iii)	octahedral	(1)	
	90°	(1)	2
5 (b) (iv)	trigonal bipyramidal	(1)	
	90°	(1)	
	120°	(1)	3

Question	Answer		Marks
5 (c)	van der Waals' attractions	(1)	
	electronegativity difference between H and S	(1)	
	H—S bonds polar	(1)	
	dipole–dipole attractions	(1)	4
			Total 19
6 (a)	Ne placed at Z = 10 and above Ar	(1)	
	Mg placed at Z = 12 and above Na, below Si	(1)	
	S placed at Z = 16 below P and above Si	(1)	
	K placed at Z = 19 below Na	(1)	4
6 (b)	Ne: electrons in a shell closer to nucleus	(1)	
	and less shielded	(1)	
	Mg: more protons than Na	(1)	
	same shielding	(1)	
	S: last electron paired in 3p	(1)	
	repulsion between electrons in pair	(1)	
	K: electrons in 4s shells	(1)	
	more shielded by 3 inner shells	(1)	8
			Total 12
7 (a)	Mg and Na both metals	(1)	
	metal–metal bonding in Mg stronger	(1)	
	2+ ions and more delocalised electrons	(1)	3
7 (b)	Al metal	(1)	
	Si macromolecular	(1)	
	Si atoms joined by covalent bonds	(1)	
	covalent bonds need more energy to break than metallic bonds	(1)	4
7 (c)	all are molecular	(1)	
	van der Waals' forces between molecules	(1)	
	strongest for largest molecules	(1)	
	P_4 smaller than S_8 larger than Cl_2	(1)	4
7 (d)	free atoms	(1)	
	van der Waals' forces between atoms	(1)	
	very weak	(1)	
	atoms small and difficult to polarise	(1)	4
			Total 15
8 (a)	% hydrogen = 100 – 85.7 = 14.3	(1)	
	carbon hydrogen		
	85.7/12 14.3/1		
	= 7.14 = 14.3	(1)	
	simplest ratio by mole is 1:2 so empirical formula = CH_2	(1)	
	mass of CH_2 = 14 M_r = 56		
	56/14 = 4		
	molecular formula = 4 × empirical formula = C_4H_8	(1)	4

Question	Answer		Marks
8 (b)	2-methylpentane	(1)	
	C_6H_{14}	(1)	
	alkanes	(1)	3
8 (c)			
	1-chloropropane (1) 2-chloropropane (1)		
	position isomerism (1)		5
			Total 12
9 (a)	$C_8H_{18} + 12.5O_2 \rightarrow 8CO_2 + 9H_2O$ correct species	(1)	
	balanced	(1)	2
9 (b) (i)	$CH_3SH + 3O_2 \rightarrow CO_2 + 2H_2O + SO_2$	(1)	1
9 (b) (ii)	$CaO + SO_2 \rightarrow CaSO_3$	(1)	
	powdered CaO injected into exhaust gases before release to atmosphere	(1)	2
9 (b) (iii)	prevents acid rain	(1)	
	CO_2 released when CaO made (lots of additional correct answers)	(1)	2
			Total 7
10 (a)	general formula	(1)	
	each member differs from the next by one CH_2 group	(1)	2
10 (b)	C_8H_{18}	(1)	
	$C_{10}H_{22}$	(1)	2
10 (c) (i)	thermal	(1)	
	high temperature	(1)	
	pressure above atmospheric	(1)	3
10 (c) (ii)	incomplete reaction	(1)	
	reaction to produce ethene instead of propene	(1)	2
10 (d) (i)	$C_9H_{20} \rightarrow C_3H_6 + C_6H_{14}$	(1)	1
10 (d) (ii)	mass of propene × 100/mass nonane	(1)	
	= 42 × 100/128 = 32.8%	(1)	2
10 (d) (iii)	make use of the other products	(1)	
	e.g. find a sales outlet for the other products	(1)	2
			Total 14
11 (a) (i)	the less viscous *light* crude must contain a higher proportion		
	of smaller molecules	(1)	
	because the intermolecular forces are weaker	(1)	2
11 (a) (ii)	*light* will be more expensive	(1)	
	smaller hydrocarbons are more in demand as fuel for vehicles	(1)	2

Question	Answer		Marks
11 (b)	$C_6H_{14} + 9\frac{1}{2}O_2 \rightarrow 6CO_2 + 7H_2O$	(1)	
	$C_9H_{20} + 14O_2 \rightarrow 9CO_2 + 10H_2O$	(1)	
	$C_{12}H_{26} + 18\frac{1}{2}O_2 \rightarrow 12CO_2 + 13H_2O$	(1)	
	smokiness = incomplete combustion	(1)	
	forming more carbon instead of carbon dioxide	(1)	
	as the number of carbon atoms increases,	(1)	
	the amount of oxygen required increases	(1)	
	the supply of oxygen is fixed	(1)	
	so incomplete combustion occurs more with the larger alkanes	(1)	9
11 (c)	$C_{15}H_{32} \rightarrow C_8H_{18} + 2C_2H_4 + C_3H_6$		
	species	(1)	
	balanced	(1)	2
11 (d)	$N_2 + O_2 \rightarrow 2NO$	(1)	
	energy for this reaction is supplied by the spark/ignition	(1)	
	$2NO + O_2 \rightarrow 2NO_2$	(1)	
	in a catalytic converter or Pt/Pd/Rh	(1)	
	$2NO + 2CO \rightarrow N_2 + 2CO_2$	(1)	5
11 (e)	sulfur dioxide formed by the combustion of sulfur-containing impurities in coal	(1)	
	removed by reaction with basic or alkaline substances such as calcium oxide	(1)	
	$CaO + SO_2 \rightarrow CaSO_3$	(1)	3
			Total 23

The table below highlights aspects of *How Science Works* in the exemplar questions.

Question	How Science Works
3	use of experimental data
4	interpretation of data
7	interpretation of data
8	empirical formulae calculations (data from experiment)
9 (b) (iii)	environmental considerations
10 (d) (iii)	posing scientific questions
11 (b)	looking for links in observations
11 (d)/(e)	environmental

Glossary

acid rain	contains quantities of carbonic, nitric and sulfuric acids
atomic (proton) number (Z)	the number of protons in the nucleus of an atom
Avogadro constant (L)	6.022×10^{23} particles mol^{-1}
catalytic cracking	occurs when the energy required for bond breaking in hydrocarbons is provided by heat, in the presence of a catalyst (compare with *thermal cracking*)
chain isomers	structural isomers which occur when there are two or more ways of arranging the carbon skeleton of a molecule
concentration	$\dfrac{\text{number of moles of solute}}{\text{volume of solution in dm}^3}$ with units mol dm^{-3}
co-ordinate bond	a covalent bond formed when the pair of electrons originate from one atom
covalent bond	a shared pair of electrons
cracking	occurs when large alkanes are broken into smaller molecules
displayed formula	shows all the bonds present in a molecule
electronegativity	the power of an atom to attract the shared electrons in a covalent bond
empirical formula	the simplest ratio of atoms of each element in a compound
energy levels	the specific values of energy that an electron may have in an atom
enthalpy change (ΔH)	the amount of heat energy released or absorbed when a chemical or physical change occurs at constant pressure
enthalpy of fusion	the enthalpy required to change one mole of a solid into a liquid, i.e. $X(s) \rightarrow X(l)$
enthalpy of vaporisation	the enthalpy required to change one mole of a liquid into a gas, i.e. $X(l) \rightarrow X(g)$
first ionisation energy	the enthalpy change for the removal of one mole of electrons from one mole of atoms of an element in the gas phase, i.e. $X(g) \rightarrow X^+(g) + e^-$
functional group	an atom or group of atoms which, when present in different molecules, causes them to have similar chemical properties
functional group isomers	structural isomers which contain different functional groups
giant ionic lattice	see *ionic crystal*
giant metallic lattice	see *metallic crystal*
greenhouse gases	gases in the atmosphere which absorb infra-red radiation (e.g. water vapour, carbon dioxide, methane and ozone)
homologous series	a family of organic molecules which all contain the same functional group, but have an increasing number of carbon atoms
hydrogen bonding	an intermolecular force between the lone pair on an electronegative atom (N, O or F) and a hydrogen atom bonded to such an electronegative atom
ideal gas	one that obeys the ideal gas equation, $pV = nRT$
ionic bond	the electrostatic force of attraction between oppositely charged ions
ionic crystal	a lattice of positive and negative ions bound together by electrostatic attractions

ion	an atom or group of atoms which has lost or gained one or more electrons, giving it a positive or negative charge
isomers	molecules with the same chemical formula but in which the atoms are arranged differently (see *structural isomerism* and *stereoisomerism*)
isotopes	atoms of the same element with the same atomic number but different mass numbers
macromolecular (giant) crystal	a large, covalently-bonded lattice structure
macromolecule	a large molecule
mass number (A)	the total number of protons and neutrons in the nucleus of one atom of the element
metallic bonding	electrostatic attraction between metal ions and delocalised electrons
metallic crystal	a lattice of metal ions surrounded by delocalised electrons
mole	a quantity of particles (1 mol is 6.022×10^{23} particles)
molecular crystal	a lattice of covalent molecules held together by weak intermolecular forces
molecular formula	the actual number of atoms of each element in a molecule
neutral atoms	contain an equal number of positively charged protons and negatively charged electrons
orbitals	volumes in space around the nucleus within which electrons are most likely to be found
percentage atom economy	$\dfrac{\text{mass of desired product}}{\text{total mass of reactants}} \times 100$ it is a measure of how much of a desired product in a reaction is formed from the reactants
percentage yield	$\dfrac{\text{actual mass of product}}{\text{maximum theoretical mass of products}} \times 100$ it is a practical measure of the efficiency of a reaction
polarity	the displacement of electron density (formation of an electric dipole) in a covalent bond, or in a molecule, due to a difference in electronegativity
position isomers	structural isomers which have the same carbon skeleton and the same functional group, but in which the functional group is joined at different places on the carbon skeleton
relative atomic mass (A_r)	$\dfrac{\text{average mass of one atom of an element}}{\frac{1}{12} \times \text{the mass of one atom of } {}^{12}\text{C}}$
relative molecular mass (M_r)	$\dfrac{\text{average mass of one molecule}}{\frac{1}{12} \times \text{the mass of one atom of } {}^{12}\text{C}}$
saturated hydrocarbons	contain carbon–carbon single bonds as well as carbon–hydrogen bonds
square planar	the spatial arrangement of a central atom surrounded by four atoms situated at the corners of a square

stereoisomerism	occurs when molecules with the same structural formula have the bonds arranged differently in space (see *Collins Student Support Materials: Unit 2 - Chemistry in Action,* section 3.2.9, and *Unit 4 - Kinetics, Equilibria and Organic Chemistry,* section 3.4.4)
structural formula	shows the unique arrangement of atoms in a molecule in a simplified form without showing all the bonds
structural isomers	compounds with the same molecular formula but different structures
structural isomerism	occurs when the component atoms are arranged differently in molecules having the same molecular formula
thermal cracking	occurs when the energy required for bond breaking in hydrocarbons is provided by heat alone (compare with *catalytic cracking*)

Index

Notes